# Echoes of the Gods: Rediscovering the Heroes and Deities of Ancient Egypt

Myrddin Sage

Published by Myrddin Sage, 2024.

While every precaution has been taken in the preparation of this book, the publisher assumes no responsibility for errors or omissions, or for damages resulting from the use of the information contained herein.

ECHOES OF THE GODS: REDISCOVERING THE HEROES AND DEITIES OF ANCIENT EGYPT

**First edition. August 3, 2024.**



ISBN: 979-8227969040

Written by Myrddin Sage.

# Also by Myrddin Sage

Mythic Japan: Unlocking the Legends of Gods and Heroes
Echoes of Enchantment: Navigating the Magic of Celtic Mythology
Echoes of Valhalla: Unveiling the Modern Wisdom of Norse Myths
Gods Among Us: The Power and Intrigue of Roman Mythology
The Sword and the Sage: Unveiling the Truth of Excalibur and Merlin
Myth Unleashed: Rediscovering the Legends of Hercules and the
Pantheon
Echoes of the Gods: Rediscovering the Heroes and Deities of Ancient
Egypt

# Table of Contents

# Echoes of the Gods: Rediscovering the Heroes and Deities of Ancient Egypt

## Dive Into the Mythical World of Ancient Egypt and Unlock the Secrets of its Gods and Heroes Today

# Preface

**"***The past is never dead. It's not even past.***" - *William Faulkner.*

In this intriguing exploration titled ***Echoes of the Gods: Rediscovering the Heroes and Deities of Ancient Egypt***, we delve into the enchanting world of ancient Egyptian mythology with a fresh perspective, aiming to bring the gods and heroes of yesteryears alive in the minds and hearts of modern readers. This book seeks to bridge the gap between historical scholarship and engaging storytelling through vivid narratives and thoughtful analysis.

My journey into writing this book began during a dusty summer spent navigating the vast halls of the Cairo Museum. Amidst artifacts that whispered secrets of millennia, I realized how tales of gods like Osiris and heroes like Horus resonate with timeless themes of life, death, and rebirth. Yet, despite their richness, these stories are often buried under academic jargon or lost in esoteric translations. This sparked a desire to present these myths in a way that feels alive, relevant, and accessible to everyone, not just scholars.

Imagine walking through an ancient temple, feeling the cool stone beneath your fingers, hearing the echo of priestly chants while inhaling the faint scent of incense that seems almost ingrained in the walls. This is the kind of sensory journey I wish to offer you. Many have shared their frustrations about dry academic texts that feel more like reading a refrigerator manual than engaging with vibrant deities whose stories shaped an entire civilization. It is for them—and for you—that I wrote this book.

I am deeply grateful to a circle of esteemed Egyptologists and passionate mythologists whose insights have been instrumental in shaping this narrative. Their rigorous scholarship provided a solid foundation upon which I could build stories that educate and entertain.

To all who embark on reading this book, thank you for allowing me to guide you through the mystical landscapes of ancient Egypt. Your curiosity and enthusiasm make this journey worthwhile. Whether you are a seasoned fan of mythology or a newcomer eager to explore ancient cultures, there is something in these pages for you.

By the end of this book, expect to be informed and enchanted by the rich tapestry of myths that played a crucial role in one of history's most fascinating civilizations. You will gain not just knowledge but experience—a vivid imagining of what it might have felt like to live amidst the gods and heroes of ancient Egypt. This book is not just a collection of stories but a journey of enlightenment that will deepen your understanding of ancient Egyptian culture and mythology.

Thank you for choosing to explore these age-old echoes with me. Let us turn the page together and rediscover the wonders that await in ancient Egyptian myths.

# Chapter 1: Living Legends - Unearthing the Vibrancy of Ancient Egyptian Myths

In the dim light of a late afternoon, the dusty library of Cairo University held more than rows of ancient texts; it cradled centuries of myths and truths intertwined like the roots of an old sycamore tree. Sarah, a young archaeology student, tiptoed between the stacks, her fingers tracing the spines of books that whispered secrets of a time long past. She was searching for something – not just knowledge but understanding, a connection to the ancient world that seemed so distant yet vibrantly alive in these pages.

Her focus today was on Egyptian mythology, its relevance not buried in history but pulsing in the present. The tales were not just stories; they were reflections of life's eternal dance with themes as relevant now as they were thousands of years ago – love, betrayal, power. As she flipped through a particularly worn leather-bound book, she paused on a passage about Isis and Osiris – a story steeped in love and resurrection. It made her think about her own struggles with loss and renewal. How often had she sought to piece together the fragments of her life?

Outside, the sun began its descent, casting long shadows across the library floor that seemed to reach toward Sarah like fingers from the past. She could almost hear the bustle of an ancient marketplace and smell the incense burning in a temple ceremony; such was the power of these myths to transport her across millennia.

Dr. Ahmed, her mentor and guide in this academic journey, interrupted her reverie. "Finding what you need?" he asked with a knowing smile.

"Yes," she replied, "it's fascinating how these myths are not just relics but living stories that still speak to us about human nature."

"Exactly," Dr. Ahmed nodded, his eyes gleaming with enthusiasm.

"They teach us about resilience, about navigating life's complexities with wisdom and courage."

As Sarah resumed her reading, she delved deeper into stories in which gods and mortals faced trials that tested their strength and spirit. In these narratives, she saw reflections of her own life—moments where she felt betrayed or empowered, times when love was both a source of pain and profound growth.

The room grew quieter as the evening deepened; only the soft rustling of pages filled the air. Sarah felt a kinship with those who had lived so long ago yet experienced emotions akin to hers. It was comforting and unsettling all at once. This timeless human experience is shared across centuries through tales told by firelight under starry skies.

Why do we find echoes of our own lives in these ancient myths?

What does it tell us about our shared humanity?

# Unveil the Timeless Echoes of Ancient Egypt

Ancient Egyptian mythology, often viewed through the lens of distant scholarly analysis, is ripe for a vivid reawakening in our modern consciousness. Far from being mere relics of the past, these myths are pulsating stories teeming with themes and emotions that mirror our contemporary lives. In this opening exploration, we delve into why these age-old tales of gods, heroes, and mortals are not just historical footnotes but are narratives bursting with life, offering insights and reflections pertinent to today's world. They are not just stories of the past but mirrors reflecting our present reality.

## The Living Breath of Myths

Imagine the myths of Ancient Egypt as living entities; they breathe, they influence, and they resonate deeply with the human experience.

Each story, from the sun god Ra's daily rebirth to Isis' profound love and cunning, is imbued with elements that transcend time—power struggles, redemption arcs, and quests for eternal life. These stories are not locked in the past; they evolve with us and offer new meanings as we navigate our modern lives. They are not static tales but dynamic narratives that continue to shape our understanding of the world.

## A Mirror to Our World

Why do these ancient narratives matter now? They provide a mirror reflecting our societal dilemmas— leadership, justice, betrayal, and the eternal quest for meaning. By reconnecting with these myths, we engage in a dialogue with history that enriches our understanding of the past and the present. This chapter aims to bridge the gap between ancient text and contemporary relevance, highlighting how these enduring tales shed light on universal human experiences.

## Storytelling as a Dynamic Art

Mythology should be celebrated as a field of study and as a vibrant form of storytelling that can captivate and inspire. By exploring key themes such as life, death, power, betrayal, and love within these myths, we uncover the artistry with which these narratives were crafted. This approach transforms our engagement with mythology from static reading to an immersive experience that vividly brings the rich tapestry of Ancient Egyptian culture to life.

## Cultivating Appreciation Through Dynamic Narrative

AS WE PROGRESS THROUGH this narrative journey, we aim to cultivate a deeper appreciation for mythology's role in shaping cultural identity. Understanding these stories in their full dynamism allows us to appreciate their historical significance and their ongoing impact on literature, art, and philosophy. This chapter sets the stage for a transformative exploration that connects us with the ancient world meaningfully and engagingly.

By approaching Ancient Egyptian myths as dynamic stories filled with complex characters and intricate plots rather than static academic records, we open ourselves up to a world where gods walk among mortals, and each myth carries a profound emotional truth relevant to our lives. Join us as we unearth the vibrancy of these ancient narratives and rediscover their relevance in our modern world.

This journey through "Echoes of the Gods" is more than just a rediscovery; it's an invitation to experience mythology as a living form that continues to inspire awe and wonder across ages. Let us rekindle our connection with these legendary figures as distant icons and vibrant entities whose stories resonate deeply with our human saga.

# Understanding the Contemporary Resonance of Ancient Egyptian Myths

Ancient Egyptian myths, often envisioned as ornate hieroglyphs on monumental temples, are not just relics of a distant past but are vibrant narratives that still echo today's societal issues. These stories were not merely for entertainment; they encapsulated the Egyptians' values, struggles, and aspirations. For example, the myth of Isis and Osiris tackles themes of love, betrayal, and the quest for justice. These themes are prevalent in many of today's famous stories.

In an analogy, consider the myths as mirrors reflecting the image of ancient society and the ongoing human saga. Just as a mirror reflects our present image irrespective of age, these myths reflect timeless human emotions and conflicts that resonate with modern audiences. They show that the fundamental aspects of human nature have remained consistent over millennia—love, ambition, jealousy, and resilience.

These narratives provide a framework for understanding how ancient people interpreted the world around them. Through myths, we see how the Egyptians personified natural elements into gods and goddesses, embedding them with human traits to explain natural phenomena and life events. This anthropomorphic portrayal helps modern individuals connect personally with these ancient stories, seeing reflections of their own lives and struggles.

The power of myth lies in its ability to transcend time. Egyptian myths, like those of Osiris, teach about the cycles of life and death, offering comfort and understanding about mortality, a topic as relevant now as it was thousands of years ago. The story of Osiris's resurrection assures us of the possibility of life after death, providing a form of solace and hope that many seek today.

Egyptian myths resonate with contemporary issues and emotions, proving they are much more than historical artifacts.

## Discovering Life, Death, Power, Betrayal, and Love

THE FABRIC OF EGYPTIAN mythology is woven with the themes of life, death, power, betrayal, and love—elements that define the human experience. Each myth carries these themes across time, imparting wisdom and insights into the nature of existence. Take, for instance, the tale of Isis and Osiris, where love and betrayal are central themes leading to Osiris's ultimate rebirth and immortality.

*Life and death are not just events but profound elements explored* extensively in Egyptian mythology. These myths often depict the afterlife as a mirror of the earthly life, suggesting a continuity that comforts the living with a promise of permanence beyond death. This portrayal helps individuals grapple with mortality and the mystery of what lies beyond.

Power dynamics within these myths reveal the complexities of authority and governance, as seen in the story of Set betraying Osiris to usurp his throne. This narrative explores the corrupting influence of power and the resilience needed to reclaim justice, mirroring modern political dramas and conflicts.

Exploring these themes through mythical narratives adds depth to our understanding of ancient Egyptian culture. It shows us that the ancients grappled with many of the same questions and challenges we face today.

*Could understanding these ancient narratives about power and betrayal shed light on our current social and political dilemmas?*

# Appreciating Mythology as Dynamic Storytelling

MYTHOLOGY, MAINLY EGYPTIAN mythology, is a collection of stories from a bygone era and a dynamic form of storytelling that brings ancient cultures to life. These myths were the Egyptians' way of making sense of the complexities surrounding them, packaged in narratives filled with drama, intrigue, and metaphysical questions.

Just as painters use a canvas to bring their artistic visions to life, ancient storytellers use myths to paint pictures of life's truths.

These stories are crafted to be engaging and thought-provoking, designed to be passed down through generations, each retelling adding a new layer of interpretation and relevance.

The dynamic nature of mythology is evident in how these stories adapt over time, influencing modern literature, movies, and even comic books. This adaptability underscores the versatility of myth as a storytelling form that is not only educational but also entertaining.

By delving into Egyptian mythology, we gain insights into how ancient people understood their world and managed life's unpredictabilities. These stories, with their gods and mortals, act almost as historical documents that offer a glimpse into the ancient Egyptians' everyday lives, hopes, and fears.

*Understanding Egyptian mythology as living stories helps us appreciate it as a form of dynamic storytelling that vividly brings ancient culture to life, intertwining past lessons with the realities of the present.*

As we delve into the mythological tapestry of Ancient Egypt, it becomes clear that these stories are more than just relics of the past. They are vibrant, living narratives that continue to speak powerfully about the universal themes of life, death, power, betrayal, and love. By presenting these myths as dynamic and relevant, we preserve their richness and allow them to resonate with modern audiences, offering fresh perspectives on contemporary issues.

*Understanding how Egyptian myths transcend time* shows us that the emotions and dilemmas faced by the ancients are not so different from our own. This connection forms a bridge across millennia, reminding us of the shared human experience that underlies all culture and history.

*Discovering the elements of life and mythology* in these stories encourages us to reflect on our own lives. Through the trials and triumphs of gods and heroes, we find mirrors of our struggles and victories, making ancient wisdom accessible and applicable daily.

*Appreciating mythology as a dynamic storytelling form* brings ancient culture vividly to life. It transforms our engagement with history, turning it from a static academic study into an active, personal experience. This approach deepens our understanding and enhances our appreciation of Ancient Egyptian civilization, making it more tangible and immediate.

As we progress in this journey, each chapter will build on these foundations, exploring individual myths and characters in greater depth. You will discover the rich symbolism and profound philosophy of these ancient narratives and their relevance to modern life.

By embracing these timeless stories, we invite wisdom, inspiration, and a deeper connection to the past into our lives today. Let us continue to explore these legendary narratives together, uncovering the lessons they hold for us now and in the future. Join me in rediscovering the heroes and deities of Ancient Egypt, and let their stories enrich your understanding of both the ancient world and your own place within it.

# Chapter 2: Gods Among Us - The Divine Role of the Pharaohs

The sun was a fierce overseer in the clear sky above Thebes, its rays unforgiving as they beat down on the sandstone walls of the temple. Amidst this relentless heat, Merenptah, a young scribe of considerable repute, found himself poring over scrolls that smelled of age and wisdom. His fingers traced the hieroglyphs with reverence, each symbol a gateway to divine secrets.

Today, he was absorbed in texts about the Pharaohs—not just as rulers but as gods in human form. This concept fascinated him deeply; these men walked between two worlds, holding sway over the fertile lands of Egypt and the ethereal realms of the gods.

In his small chamber filled with papyrus and ink pots, Merenptah's mind wandered to Pharaoh Seti I, his divine lineage granting him powers beyond mortal ken. Seti I was both father and god to his people, his decrees shaping the land as if he wielded the staff of Osiris himself. How profound must it have been to see one's king in such light — a being who could command both army and rain?

Outside, life moved with the usual rhythm:

- Priests shuffled along stone corridors discussing theological matters.
- Laborers sang work songs that echoed off granite walls.
- Market vendors shouted their wares.

*Yet here, inside these quiet walls, lay truths that bound all those lives together under divine rule.*

Merenptah's thoughts were interrupted by a sudden gust that fluttered through his open window — perhaps Amun himself reminding him of his mortal place. He smiled slightly at this thought before returning to his study. The relationship between governance and worship intrigued him, as well as how seamlessly politics and faith intertwined under the Pharaoh's dual role. It wasn't merely about power but cosmic order, Ma'at — keeping the balance between chaos and harmony.

As dusk approached and painted everything with an orange hue softer than dawn's first light, Merenptah wondered about those ancient myths where Pharaohs stood central among gods. What lessons did they hold for him? For all who still believed in their enduring power?

*Could understanding their divine attributes offer insights into their eternal influence over Egypt's sands?*

# Unveiling the Divine: The Pharaohs of Ancient Egypt

In the tapestry of ancient Egyptian civilization, the figure of the Pharaoh stands out as a pivotal force, embodying both the might of kingship and the charisma of divinity. This dual role was not merely a title or a status but a fundamental element that shaped every aspect of Egyptian life—from governance and culture to religion and mythology. As we delve into this chapter, we will explore how the Pharaohs, revered as gods on earth, directed their time's spiritual and political currents.

## The God-Kings of the Nile

The Pharaoh's unique position as both a ruler and a divine entity is a concept that might seem foreign or even unbelievable to us today.

Yet, this was an accepted reality for the ancient Egyptians that influenced their expectations of leadership and justice. The divine right of Pharaohs wasn't just about authoritarian rule. Still, it was deeply interwoven with their responsibility to maintain Ma'at—the cosmic order and balance critical to the welfare of the state and its people.

# Governance Infused with Divinity

One must recognize how this blend of divine mandate and royal authority impacted governance. The laws they enacted and their decisions were considered extensions of divine will, necessitating a harmonious balance that was believed to be ordained by the gods.

This perspective transformed leadership from mere administration to a sacred duty. Pharaohs were seen as shepherds of their people's moral and spiritual well-being.

# Myths That Governed a Civilization

The myths surrounding these divine rulers are stories and reflections of deeply held beliefs and cultural paradigms. By analyzing specific myths where Pharaohs are central figures, we understand how their godly attributes were perceived and propagated among the masses. These narratives served as religious instruction and legitimized the Pharaohs' rule, reinforcing their status as earthly manifestations of divine power.

*Understanding this dual identity* is crucial for anyone seeking a deeper comprehension of how mythology and governance intertwined in ancient Egypt. It provides a clearer picture of why Pharaohs could command such extraordinary loyalty and reverence, which ensured stability and continuity in Egyptian society.

Reflecting on these themes promises to explore a fascinating aspect of ancient history. It offers us timeless lessons on leadership and moral responsibility. As we proceed, remember that our journey through these ancient narratives is more than an academic exercise; it is a quest to uncover enduring truths about power, faith, and human nature within these age-old tales.

By embracing this understanding, we pay homage to their remarkable civilization and enrich our perspectives on leadership, divinity, and human aspirations. In doing so, we continue to learn from those who once walked along the Nile under the watchful eyes of gods they believed walked among them.

# Exploring the Significance of Pharaohs as Both Rulers and Divine Representatives

In the tapestry of ancient Egyptian civilization, the Pharaoh was not just a ruler but a pivotal religious icon. This dual role was rooted deeply in the Egyptian belief system, where the Pharaoh was seen as a direct descendant of the gods, primarily the god Horus during their reign and Osiris in the afterlife. This belief underscored the Pharaoh's unique position as a divine representative and a mortal leader.

Imagine a bridge spanning two worlds, one divine and the other human. The Pharaoh was like this bridge, connecting the gods to the people. The divine will was understood through him, and societal norms were established. This role as a bridge made the Pharaoh an indispensable part of Egyptian spiritual and daily life.

Their governance was heavily influenced by their perceived divinity. Laws and decrees could be seen as not just royal commands but as ordained by the gods. This divine endorsement gave the Pharaoh's decisions a weight that could not be easily contested, weaving their rule into the very spiritual fabric of society.

A Pharaoh's decision was imbued with spiritual significance, turning mundane governance into a series of divine acts. This intertwining of the secular and the religious in the Pharaoh's role helped stabilize and justify their rule. It wasn't simply about leading the people; it was about guiding them through a world that reflected the gods' will.

*The Pharaoh was both a king and a god, a dual role that shaped every aspect of ancient Egyptian culture.*

# Examining the Impact of the Dual Role on Governance and Religious Practices

The Pharaoh's dual role as both a secular leader and a divine figure had profound implications for governance and religious practices in ancient Egypt. Integrating divine authority into political leadership meant that governance was not merely a temporal affair but was entwined with the nation's spiritual health.

In the governance structure, this dual role manifested through rituals and state decrees that were often religious. Festivals, temple constructions, and religious ceremonies were not just acts of devotion but also tools of statecraft. They reinforced the Pharaoh's divine status and, by extension, his political authority.

The line between religion and politics was blurred by positioning the Pharaoh as a divine entity. ***Religious leaders often held significant political power***, and vice versa; priests were key advisers to the Pharaoh. This symbiosis between the temple and the throne centralized power and unified the state under a shared religious and political culture.

What if governance itself was seen as a religious ritual? Every law and every decision from the Pharaoh was a step towards cosmic harmony dictated by divine foresight. This perspective transformed the citizens' view of authority, embedding their political obedience within their religious devotion.

The impact of this dual role is evident in the extensive iconography and monumental architecture that celebrated divine kingship, creating a legacy that has endured millennia.

***Could understand this intertwined relationship between divine command and royal decree change how we view leadership today?***

## Analyzing Specific Myths to Understand Pharaohs' Divine Attributes

The myths surrounding the Pharaohs are not just stories; they are reflections of the divine expectations placed upon these god-kings.

Analyzing these myths provides insights into how the divine attributes of the Pharaohs were communicated and understood.

For instance, the myth of Osiris, who was resurrected to become the ruler of the afterlife, parallels the Pharaoh's role as a renewer of life and a guarantor of the afterlife. This myth reinforced the Pharaoh's role as a steward of both the land of the living and the realm of the dead.

Consider a Pharaoh as a star in the sky—a fixed point of light guiding the ancient Egyptians through seasons and rituals. This celestial analogy helps us understand the Pharaoh's role as a constant divine presence in the people's lives, guiding them just as the stars guide sailors at night.

The story of Isis and Osiris, where order is restored through divine intervention, also mirrors the Pharaoh's duty to maintain Ma'at (order, balance, and justice) in the kingdom. This myth emphasized the Pharaoh's responsibility to uphold cosmic balance, further solidifying their image as divine agents on earth.

By exploring these myths, we delve deeper into the understanding of the Pharaoh as more than just a ruler; they were a central figure in ancient Egypt's spiritual and mythological landscape.

*These myths not only entertain but also highlight the divine nature of the Pharaohs' rule, tying together their roles as both secular leaders and religious icons.*

Throughout this exploration of the Pharaohs' divine and regal roles, we've unearthed a profound understanding of their dual existence.

These leaders were more than mere rulers; they were incarnations of gods, vested with responsibilities that spanned the spiritual and the administrative realms. This blend of authority reinforced their control and profoundly influenced Egyptian culture and religion.

*Pharaohs, as divine entities,* significantly shaped the governance of ancient Egypt. Their perceived godliness ensured an almost unchallengeable societal position, intertwining politics with religious devotion. This unity was vital for maintaining order and harmony across the Nile's fertile banks. By embodying gods, Pharaohs could command incredible loyalty and dedication, factors essential for the stability and longevity of their reigns.

The impact on *religious practices* was equally profound. Temples were not just places of worship but also centers of political power, reinforcing the divine right to rule bestowed upon the Pharaohs. Rituals and ceremonies often emphasized the Pharaoh's central role in maintaining Ma'at, or cosmic order, echoing their indispensability to their people and the gods they represented.

By analyzing specific myths, we see these leaders as historical figures and pivotal characters in tales that have shaped an entire civilization's worldview. The stories of gods and Pharaohs are intertwined, reinforcing the sacred nature of the Pharaoh's role.

Through myths, we understand not just the beliefs of ancient Egyptians but also their societal structure, where the divine right of kings was unquestioned and paramount.

Recognizing the Pharaohs' dual roles enriches our comprehension of Egyptian mythology and its lasting legacy. It explains the profound reverence they commanded and why their authority was politically and spiritually absolute. This insight is not just academic; it invites us to reflect on how leadership is viewed in our cultures and how it shapes our values and governance.

By delving into these ancient narratives, we gain knowledge and a broader perspective on power, divinity, and human society. Let us carry forward this understanding, appreciating the intricate tapestry of history and mythology that ancient Egypt offers. This exploration is a testament to their enduring allure and the lessons they continue to teach us about the interplay between the mortal and the divine.

# Chapter 3: Beyond Death - The Egyptian Vision of the Afterlife

The sun was already high over the banks of the Nile, casting a sharp glare on the water that made the fishermen squint as they cast their nets. Amara walked through the market in the nearby village, her thoughts as tangled as the vibrant fabrics piled high on the vendors' tables. She was a potter by trade, shaping clay into vessels and figurines that might someday accompany her neighbors into the afterlife. The belief in a life beyond death permeated every aspect of Egyptian life, from grand pyramids to humble household shrines.

Amara's fingers brushed against a small amulet of Anubis, guardian of the dead. It reminded her how deeply her people valued guidance and protection in their journey to what lay beyond this earthly existence. The afterlife was not a mere shadowy existence but a continuation of life on earth, filled with possibilities and challenges. This belief shaped their burial practices and how they lived each day.

Turning away from the market stalls, Amara headed towards the riverbank, where she often found clay for her pottery. The earth was cool under her bare feet, rich with nutrients carried by the annual flooding of the Nile. It struck her then how this river, giver of life and sustainer of crops, was also central to their beliefs about rebirth and renewal in death.

As she dug her hands into the moist soil, scooping up handfuls to feel its texture between her fingers, Amara thought about how this clay would soon be shaped into objects for both daily use and burial rites. These artifacts would carry forward messages and values through time, an unspoken dialogue between generations about what mattered most to them: continuity, remembrance, and respect for tradition.

She paused in her work as a group of children ran past along the riverbank, chasing a wayward goat. Their laughter echoed across the water's surface, a reminder that life here embraced joy and reverence in equal measure.

Amara looked back at her gathered clay and contemplated how each piece she created would one day witness someone's journey into eternity. What stories would these silent objects tell? How would future generations interpret these symbols crafted by hands like hers? And could they ever truly understand our deep connection to an afterlife so vividly imagined yet unseen?

## Unveiling Eternity: Ancient Egypt's Vision of Life Beyond Death

WHEN WE THINK ABOUT the afterlife, our modern minds often entertain visions of a final destination—either a place of eternal rest or punishment. However, the ancient Egyptians had a radically different perspective. They saw the afterlife as another phase of existence, seamlessly continuing from their earthly life. This chapter delves into how this belief was central to their spirituality and a driving force in their daily lives and monumental burial practices.

The Egyptians' elaborate preparations for death—embalming bodies, constructing grand pyramids, and filling tombs with goods and offerings—were all rooted in the expectation of life beyond death. This vision was so vivid that it shaped every aspect of their civilization, from architecture to daily routines. It underscored a unique cultural and spiritual identity. By comparing these ancient beliefs with today's views on the afterlife, we gain historical insights and a reflection on how our current beliefs shape our world.

Integrating the spiritual and the mundane in Egyptian life offers a fascinating study of how deeply culture can be imbued by religious beliefs. The pharaohs, viewed as gods themselves, were central figures not only in governance but in the spiritual health of the nation. Their tombs were designed to ensure their immortality and continued influence in the world of the living and the dead. This belief system reveals much about Egyptian values, such as justice, order, and an eternal commitment to communal prosperity.

Investigating how these ancient practices influenced daily life in Egypt reveals that preparations for death were also for life; they were an affirmation of faith in a known yet unseen world. The Egyptians lived each day with an eye toward eternity, influencing everything from their governance to personal holiness and social interactions.

This chapter explores these elements to highlight how spirituality was not a separate realm for the ancient Egyptians but a pervasive influence that touched all aspects of life. The grandeur of their burial sites and enduring rituals reflect an obsession with death and a profound commitment to life itself—both seen and unseen.

Recognizing these cultural priorities helps us appreciate why Egyptian civilization has captivated the world's imagination across millennia. Their vision of life as an eternal journey offers us timeless lessons on how beliefs can shape civilizations profoundly and enduringly.

This exploration into Egyptian views on life after death broadens our understanding of ancient cultures and invites us to reflect on our beliefs about mortality and legacy. What can we learn from the Egyptians about living a life that prepares for death? How might our own cultural practices around death inform or inspire us? As we journey through this chapter, these questions are central, aiming to connect past wisdom with modern reflections on existence beyond death.

# Exploring the Egyptian Conception of the Afterlife

THE ANCIENT EGYPTIANS viewed the afterlife as a mirror of their earthly lives, brimming with activities, responsibilities, and pleasures. Unlike many modern interpretations that focus on the afterlife as a final resting place or a realm of spiritual existence detached from physical experiences, Egyptians prepared for a continuation of life beyond death. This belief, deeply embedded in their culture, influenced every aspect of their lives, from architecture to daily rituals.

In modern times, the afterlife is often seen through an abstractionist lens. It is frequently portrayed as a spiritual realm where earthly matters dissolve, focusing more on the soul's redemption or punishment. This contrast with the Egyptian view is like comparing a river to a vast ocean; both are bodies of water, but their natures and experiences are profoundly different.

Egyptians enriched their tombs with possessions, food, and artifacts, underscoring their belief in a tangible afterlife. They saw death not as a cessation but as a transition to another phase of existence, where one would need all the possessions that were part of their earthly life. Modern views, however, often strip away these material connections, focusing instead on the ethereal aspects of existence.

This integration of life and the afterlife in Egyptian culture highlights a holistic approach to existence, where death is merely a continuation rather than an end. By understanding this, we can appreciate the depth of their connection to the afterlife, which was not just a belief but a vivid, detailed expectation of continued existence.

*The key takeaway is that Egyptians viewed the afterlife as a direct continuation of earthly life, contrasting significantly with modern perspectives that view it more abstractly.*

# Impact of Afterlife Beliefs on Egyptian Culture

THE EGYPTIANS' ANTICIPATION of life after death shaped not only their burial customs but also their daily activities. They built massive pyramids and elaborate tombs, believing that these structures would be their homes in the afterlife. This perspective made them invest immense resources and labor into building tombs that are marvels of human achievement today.

How did this belief in an elaborate afterlife influence their daily living? Egyptians lived each day with an eye toward eternity, meaning everyday activities were performed with extraordinary care and attention. Their moral and ethical decisions were often guided by how they would be judged in the afterlife, a concept documented in the Negative Confession, part of their funerary texts.

Imagine how vines grow around a sturdy tree, depending on it for support. Similarly, the Egyptians' daily lives were intricately entwined with their beliefs about the afterlife. Their views on eternal life influenced their agricultural practices, societal structures, and even the pharaoh's divine status.

Such a profound integration of belief and practice suggests that the boundary between life and death was permeable for Egyptians.

Their preparations for death were as much a part of daily life as farming the Nile's banks. This seamless integration underscores a unique worldview where life and the afterlife coexist continuously.

*Could understanding this integration lead us to reconsider how we view our own lives and legacies?*

## The Afterlife Belief Framework

*THE AFTERLIFE BELIEF Framework (ABF)* provides a structured way to understand how the ancient Egyptians' views of the afterlife influenced their culture, daily life, and burial practices. This model integrates comparative views, burial customs, and artifacts to comprehensively understand Egyptian spirituality and its practical implications.

# Comparison Segment

THE FIRST COMPONENT of the ABF compares modern and ancient Egyptian views of the afterlife. While modern interpretations often focus on ethereal or spiritual continuations devoid of physical form, the Egyptians imagined a more tangible continuation of life. This segment highlights these contrasts and draws parallels, enriching our understanding of ancient Egyptian spirituality.

# Burial Customs

THE SECOND COMPONENT delves into burial customs, examining elaborate tomb structures and the significance of funerary texts like the "Book of the Dead." These practices were not just about honoring the dead; they were a celebration of life and a meticulous preparation for the next world. The customs underscore the Egyptians' belief in an afterlife that mirrored their earthly life.

# Artifacts

THE THIRD SEGMENT FOCUSES on the artifacts in tombs, such as shabtis, canopic jars, and amulets. Each of these items had specific roles in ensuring a safe passage and a prosperous life in the afterlife. Understanding these artifacts helps reveal how deeply the Egyptians cared for the afterlife, ensuring that it was as rich and prepared as their current existence.

The dynamics of the ABF show how these components interact and depend on each other. Beliefs about the afterlife informed burial practices, which dictated the types of artifacts in tombs. This interdependency created a coherent and comprehensive cultural approach to death and the afterlife, illustrating a unique equilibrium in ancient Egyptian society.

*This framework enhances our understanding of ancient Egyptian culture. It shows how deeply intertwined their views of the afterlife were with their daily lives and societal organization.*

As we reflect on the profound insights gained from exploring the ancient Egyptian vision of the afterlife, it becomes clear how deeply their beliefs shaped their civilization. The Egyptians' view of death as merely a transition into another form of existence profoundly influenced their monumental burial practices, daily lives, and societal structures.

*The comparison between ancient Egyptian and modern perspectives on the afterlife* reveals stark contrasts. Modern views often perceive death as an end. In contrast, it was a complex journey to eternal life for the Egyptians, necessitating detailed preparations like mummification and elaborate burial rituals. This unique approach underlines a cultural fabric deeply woven with spirituality and an unshakeable belief in the continuity of life beyond death.

*The influence of these afterlife beliefs on Egyptian society* was all-encompassing. From the grand pyramids to the meticulous preservation of the body and the creation of the Book of the Dead, every aspect was designed to ensure a safe passage and a blissful existence in the next world. These practices were not mere rituals but a reflection of a worldview that saw this life and the next as deeply interconnected.

*The spiritual and cultural priorities of the Egyptians,* as illustrated through their afterlife beliefs, highlight their profound respect for cosmic order and balance, encapsulated in the concept of Ma'at. The role of deities like Osiris in judging the dead was about maintaining moral order and sustaining the universe's harmony.

This exploration invites us to consider our views on life and death. It challenges us to consider how our beliefs shape our actions and priorities. The ancient Egyptians taught us that our views on the afterlife can influence individual ethics and the entire societal structure, encouraging a life lived with purpose and preparation for what comes next.

By engaging with these timeless lessons from ancient Egypt, we gain knowledge about a fascinating ancient civilization and more profound insights into the universal questions of life, death, and what it means to live a life aligned with our deepest values and beliefs.

# Chapter 4: A Spectrum of Faith - The Diversity within Egyptian Beliefs

Sarah stood still in the cool, shadowed halls of the Cairo Museum under the steadfast gaze of stone gods and pharaohs. The soft whisper of her footsteps on the ancient marble floor starkly contrasted with the chaotic dance of thoughts in her mind. She was a doctoral student specializing in Ancient Egyptian religion, and today, she wrestled with a challenge that seemed as monumental as the pyramids themselves.

Sarah's research aimed to shatter the long-held belief in a static Egyptian religious system. Her thesis argued that this system was far from unchanging and dynamic, influenced by regional nuances and temporal shifts. Each artifact around her told stories of adaptation and change, yet convincing her skeptical peers remained daunting.

Her eyes caught the gleam of an amulet dedicated to Hathor. In one region, Hathor was revered as a goddess of music and fertility; in another, she took on roles of protection and vengeance. This duality fascinated Sarah; it embodied her argument about regional influences shaping divine characteristics.

As she moved through the museum, Sarah's mind drifted back to her recent field trip to Luxor. There, amidst the ruins that peppered the landscape like stars in a night sky, she had felt an overwhelming connection to her work. The villagers' tales of local deities had breathed life into her academic theories about temporal variations in worship.

Interrupting her reverie, a group of tourists bustled past, their guide recounting tales of ancient rituals with rehearsed flamboyance. Sarah smiled faintly; even today's narratives about Egypt were shaped by time and audience—much like the religious practices she studied.

She paused before a grand relief depicting Seti I offering incense to Osiris. It struck her how political power played into religious expression—pharaohs often aligned themselves with particular gods to legitimize their rule. This political dimension was crucial; it underscored how societal changes influenced religious practices.

As Sarah made notes on her tablet, an older man approached quietly beside her. He wore the tranquil expression of someone who had spent many years studying these relics.

"You see how alive it all is?" he asked gently after observing her work over her shoulder.

"Yes," Sarah replied earnestly. "It's like they speak to us across time."

"They do," he agreed with a nod. "And they tell us how change is constant—even in beliefs we consider immutable."

Their brief exchange reaffirmed Sarah's resolve to convey this dynamic nature in her thesis defense next week.

Leaving behind the cool confines of stone walls laden with history for Cairo's sunlit streets outside, where life buzzed relentlessly forward, seemed symbolic—a reminder that just like those ancient beliefs adapted over millennia, so must she adapt her arguments for modern academia.

Could understanding such vast historical complexities be fully achieved, or would scholars constantly grapple with new layers beneath old stones?

## Unraveling the Rich Tapestry of Ancient Egyptian Beliefs

ANCIENT EGYPT IS OFTEN envisioned as a civilization with a static, uniform pantheon of gods and goddesses, worshipped by all in a cohesive, unchanging manner throughout its history. However, this perception needs to be more accurate. In reality, the religious landscape of ancient Egypt was as diverse and dynamic as the Nile itself, adapting and evolving with each shift in political power and societal change. This chapter delves into the fascinating diversity within Egyptian religious practices, debunking the myth of a monolithic belief system and exploring how regional variations and historical contexts shaped the spiritual life of this intriguing civilization.

# The Myth of Uniformity

THE TYPICAL PORTRAYAL of Egyptian religion as a neatly organized system with clear-cut deities universally revered across the land does a disservice to the complexity of these ancient practices.

*Egyptian religious expression varied widely by region*, reflecting local traditions, environments, and political influences. For instance, whereas Osiris might be revered as a principal deity in one city, another might elevate Hathor or Sobek to supreme status.

This regional diversity indicates that ancient Egyptians adapted their religious practices to local conditions and needs, challenging the notion of a single, unchanging religious tradition.

# A Dynamic Religious Landscape

HISTORICAL CHANGES significantly influenced Egyptian religious practices. The conquests by Alexander the Great and later by the Romans introduced new deities and rituals into the Egyptian pantheon, often blended with existing beliefs. *This syncretism demonstrates the flexibility* of Egyptian religion and its capacity to integrate new elements without losing its identity. By examining these periods of cultural fusion, we gain insights into how religion was used not only for spiritual purposes but also as a tool for political consolidation and social control.

# Adapting to Societal Needs

RELIGION IN ANCIENT Egypt also evolved in response to societal changes. During times of hardship or upheaval, such as during invasions or internal strife, religious innovation or revivalism often surged. New forms of worship, sometimes focusing on apotropaic deities or those believed to offer protection, became prominent. These shifts underscore *how **ancient Egyptian religion was closely tied to its people's everyday experiences** and struggles.*

# Conclusion Preview

BY EXPLORING THESE aspects—debunking uniformity myths, investigating regional influences, and understanding adaptive practices—we see that Egyptian religion was far from static; it was a vibrant field of human expression that responded to an ever-changing world. As we continue this chapter, we will explore specific examples and how these dynamics played out across different epochs in Egyptian history.

Through this exploration, we aim to enrich our understanding of ancient Egyptian spirituality and appreciate its profound impact on how modern religions adapt and evolve over time. This journey into the past reveals timeless lessons about cultural resilience and spiritual diversity that are still relevant today.

# Exploring the Diversity of Egyptian Beliefs

THE COMMON BELIEF THAT the Egyptian religious system was unified and unchanging needs to be clarified. In reality, ancient Egyptian beliefs were as varied as the sands of the Sahara. The religion evolved over time, influenced by political changes and cultural exchanges. It was far from static; it was a dynamic, living faith that adapted to the needs and circumstances of its followers.

Imagine a river, like the Nile, which flows through varied landscapes, adapting its course in response to the terrain. Similarly, Egyptian religion flowed through the ages, changing and adapting. In different regions and other times, you could find distinct practices and deities worshipped fervently. This variability shows the adaptability and diversity of Egyptian spirituality.

For instance, the god Seth was honored in some regions as a protector and a necessary counterbalance to harmony, embodying essential chaos. In contrast, other areas depicted him as an evil figure. This shows not just geographical diversity but also the complexity of character and morality within the religion.

The archaeological and textual evidence needs to be revised to suggest a single, unchanging set of beliefs. Shifts in religious focus and deity popularity from the Old Kingdom to the Ptolemaic period clearly indicate a flexible and responsive belief system. This adaptability was vital to the religion's endurance across millennia.

*EGYPTIAN RELIGIOUS practices were not monolithic but a complex tapestry woven from diverse regional and temporal threads.*

# Regional and Temporal Variations in Egyptian Worship

THE WORSHIP OF ISIS serves as an excellent example of how regional and temporal variations influenced Egyptian mythology. Initially revered as a local goddess in the Nile Delta, Isis' worship spread across Egypt and beyond, adapting to local cultures and merging with other deities, such as the Greek goddess Demeter.

Why did Isis become so popular, and how did her image change from one locale to another? These questions reveal the fluid nature of mythology, shaped by human needs, political power, and cultural exchange. Isis' ability to embody different aspects—mother, healer, protector—made her worship adaptable to various contexts and appealing to a broad audience.

In Upper Egypt, for instance, her role as a funerary goddess was emphasized, aligning her with the local beliefs about the afterlife. This variation in worship shows how geography can influence the development of religious practices and the characteristics attributed to deities.

Changes in religious practices over time were also influenced by Egypt's interactions with neighboring cultures. The Hyksos invasion, for instance, introduced new deities and spiritual ideas that were absorbed into the existing Egyptian pantheon. This blending of beliefs demonstrates the dynamic nature of Egyptian religion, which is always evolving and integrating new elements.

Imagine a quilt being stitched together, each representing a different belief system or deity. Over time, the quilt grows, changes patterns, and adapts to new styles. This patchwork quilt represents the rich, varied tapestry of Egyptian religious life.

*How might understanding these adaptations in religious practice change our perception of ancient Egyptian society?*

# The Dynamic Nature of Egyptian Religious Practices

UNDERSTANDING THE DYNAMIC nature of Egyptian religious practices requires recognizing how they reflected and responded to societal changes. The construction of massive temples and the development of elaborate rituals were religious expressions and political acts that demonstrated the pharaoh's power and divine support.

For example, during times of strong central authority, temple construction projects were extensive, employing thousands and acting as a clear sign of the state's stability and the gods' favor. Conversely, these practices could change during periods of decline or foreign rule, adapting to the new political landscape.

An analogy to consider is that of a tree: just as a tree grows rings that reflect the conditions of each year, so too did Egyptian religion develop layers over time, each layer responding to its era's cultural and political climate.

The introduction of new deities and practices can also be seen as a response to society's needs. During times of hardship, such as drought or disease, the Egyptians turned to deities like Sekhmet, who were believed to have the power to ward off plagues and heal the sick. This flexibility in religious focus was a strength of the Egyptian belief system, allowing it to remain relevant and supportive to its people throughout various challenges.

*The diversity and adaptability of Egyptian religious practices highlight their role in responding to and shaping societal needs, demonstrating that this belief system was far from static; it was a vibrant and evolving part of Egyptian life.*

Throughout this chapter, we have unraveled the intricate tapestry that is the religious landscape of ancient Egypt. By examining Egyptian beliefs' *dynamic and ever-evolving nature*, it becomes evident that this was not a static or monolithic system. Instead, we find a rich mosaic of practices and deities, each colored by the nuances of regional and temporal contexts.

*Reflecting on this diversity, it becomes clear that Egyptian religion was highly responsive to the ebbs and flows of societal change.*

This adaptability underscores an essential aspect of human spirituality: its capacity to evolve in response to the needs and circumstances of its adherents. As we've seen, from the grand temples of Thebes to the smaller, local shrines scattered across the Nile Delta, each community had its own unique expressions of faith and ways of engaging with the divine.

Exploring these variations does more than broaden our understanding of ancient Egyptian culture; it invites us to appreciate the ***complexity and richness*** of religious expression as a whole. It challenges us to consider how our beliefs might be similarly nuanced and varied, influenced by our personal experiences and the world around us.

We open ourselves to a more flexible and compassionate view of spirituality by embracing the concept that beliefs can change and adapt. This understanding enriches our grasp of history and enhances our engagement with the present, encouraging us to recognize and respect the diverse ways in which people find meaning and purpose.

This chapter reminds us of the beauty and wisdom of acknowledging and celebrating diversity. It prompts us to reflect on our beliefs and the ways in which they might be shaped by our environment and experiences. As we move forward in this book, let us carry with us this appreciation for faith's fluid and dynamic nature, allowing it to inform our exploration of ancient Egypt's rich mythological world.

# Chapter 5: Decoding Symbols - The Art of Egyptian Mythology

In the warm gleam of the early afternoon, Cairo's bustling streets throbbed with life, a symphony of honking cars and vendors' calls. Amid this cacophony, Sarah moved with a sense of purpose that contrasted sharply with the meandering tourists around her. She was not here merely to gaze at the grandeur of ancient monuments; her mission was far more personal and pressing.

Her grandmother had often spoken of their lineage, tracing back to when their ancestors were believed to be custodians of sacred symbols in Egyptian mythology. With her grandmother's recent passing, Sarah felt a deep personal connection to these symbols, hoping they might ease the sharp sting of loss. The symbols—those intricate amulets and carvings—were not just art; they were keys to understanding her identity.

She paused before a small shop, its windows cluttered with replicas of ancient artifacts. Inside, she was drawn to a beautifully detailed depiction of an ankh—the symbol of life in Egyptian lore. As she traced its contours with her finger, she could almost hear her grandmother's voice recounting how such symbols were believed to carry the breath of life across generations.

Later that day, as the sun descended behind the pyramids, casting long shadows over the sandstone and marble, Sarah sat on a worn stone bench in the shade of a sycamore tree. She opened a book she had purchased—an illustrated guide to Egyptian myths and symbols. Each page revealed how these symbols intertwined with tales of gods and pharaohs, adding layers upon layers to stories she thought she knew.

A young boy approached shyly, his eyes wide as he pointed at the book. "Do you like stories about Horus and Set?" he asked in halting English.

"Yes," Sarah smiled warmly, touched by his curiosity. "These stories tell us more than just history; they show us how deeply our ancestors valued wisdom and courage."

As they spoke about Horus' epic battles and quests for justice—a narrative enriched by each symbol discussed—the boy's enthusiasm and eagerness to learn reminded Sarah why her journey was so important. It wasn't just about mourning or heritage; it was about passing on these tales so that they might inspire others as they had inspired her.

As dusk turned the sky from blue to shades of purple and gold near the horizon, Sarah watched lanterns twinkle in nearby cafes. She pondered how much depth these ancient symbols added to modern lives when appropriately understood—how they could still guide those who took the time to learn their meanings.

Could understanding these age-old symbols provide more than just historical insight? Could it also offer comfort or even guidance through life's uncertainties, making them not just relics of the past but tools for navigating the present?

## Unveiling the Veiled: A Journey into the Heart of Egyptian Mythology

EGYPTIAN MYTHOLOGY, with its rich tapestry of gods, goddesses, and mythical beings, offers a mesmerizing glimpse into the beliefs and values of ancient Egypt. Symbols form the backbone of these stories, each carrying profound meanings that often escape the modern eye. This chapter embarks on an exploratory journey to decode these symbols, utilizing various visual and interactive resources to enhance understanding and appreciation.

## Symbols as Gatekeepers of Myth

SYMBOLS IN EGYPTIAN mythology are not mere embellishments. They serve as gatekeepers to deeper truths and complex ideologies. From the ankh symbolizing life to the intricate depictions of Osiris representing death and resurrection, each symbol is a thread in the larger fabric of mythic narratives. Recognizing these symbols is essential for anyone seeking to truly grasp the essence of these ancient stories.

## The Power of Visual Learning

VISUAL AIDS SUCH AS detailed illustrations, diagrams, and thematic maps are crucial in bringing these abstract symbols to life. By seeing how these symbols are represented in art and architecture, one can better understand their significance within their original context. This visual approach clarifies and enriches the learning experience, making the myths more accessible and engaging.

## Interactive Exploration: A Modern Approach

IN TODAY'S DIGITAL age, interactive apps and online platforms offer new ways to engage with Egyptian mythology. These tools allow for a hands-on approach to learning, where users can explore virtual reconstructions of ancient sites or manipulate images to see different symbol layers. Such interactivity promotes a more dynamic education that appeals to diverse learning styles.

# The Layered Complexity of Mythological Symbols

BY EXAMINING CRITICAL symbols through various lenses—historical, cultural, and religious—we begin to appreciate their multifaceted roles in myths. The complexity revealed through this exploration shows that Egyptian mythology is not just a series of isolated tales but a coherent system where each symbol interlinks with others to form a complete narrative structure.

# Why This Matters Today

UNDERSTANDING THESE symbols satisfies historical curiosity and allows for a deeper appreciation of how ancient Egyptians viewed the world. This insight can inspire contemporary readers to reflect on their cultural symbols and values. Moreover, it highlights the enduring power of visual storytelling and its relevance in both ancient and modern contexts.

This chapter aims to educate and inspire by demonstrating how ancient wisdom encapsulated in symbols can be relevant and enlightening even today. Through this journey into Egyptian mythology, readers are invited to discover not just the myths themselves but also their own connections to this rich symbolic language. Engaging deeply with these symbols opens up new dimensions of understanding history, culture, and perhaps most importantly, ourselves.

# Identifying Key Symbols

TO DELVE INTO EGYPTIAN mythology, one must recognize the ankh, a symbol resembling a cross with a loop at the top. This symbol, often found in the hands of Egyptian deities, represents life and eternal existence. The ankh's pervasive presence in tomb paintings and scriptures underscores its importance to understanding the ancient Egyptians' aspirations for immortality.

Imagine a world where every gesture you make and every mark you leave tells a story about your beliefs and values. In ancient Egypt, symbols like the ankh were not mere decorations but powerful statements about life and beyond.

Another significant symbol is the Eye of Horus, which epitomizes protection and royal power. This icon, derived from the myth of Horus's eye being injured and restored, illustrates the concept of healing and protection. It was commonly used as an amulet to safeguard against evil.

The scarab beetle, depicted pushing the sun across the sky, symbolizes rebirth and the cycle of the day. Just as the beetle pushes the dung ball, creating new life, the sun's journey represents a daily rebirth and an eternal cycle of life, death, and resurrection.

*Identifying these symbols helps us understand ancient Egyptian culture's core values and beliefs.*

## Utilizing Visual and Interactive Tools

TO TRULY GRASP THE intricate meanings behind these symbols, engaging with visual and interactive tools proves invaluable. Visual aids like detailed diagrams and high-resolution images allow us to see the subtleties in Egyptian art, highlighting how symbols were integrated into daily life and monumental architecture.

Imagine holding a digital tablet that brings ancient artifacts to life, allowing you to rotate a 3D model of the Rosetta Stone or zoom in on the delicate carvings of a pharaoh's tomb. These tools make learning more engaging and provide a deeper understanding of the context in which these symbols were used.

Documentaries, offering narrated explorations of archaeological sites and museum collections, serve as windows into the past.

Expert commentary and cinematic visuals enhance our comprehension of how and why these symbols were so significant.

Interactive apps can transform learning into a dynamic activity. By interacting with the content, users can simulate the experience of decoding hieroglyphs or reconstructing broken artifacts, offering a hands-on approach to understanding ancient symbols.

*How might these tools change your perspective on the symbols you encounter in everyday life?*

# Appreciating Symbolic Complexity

UNDERSTANDING THE DEPTH and complexity of these symbols enriches our appreciation of Egyptian myths. Each symbol carried multiple layers of meaning, often interwoven with the mythology and cultural practices of the time.

# The Symbolic Framework Model

## Decoding the Language of Egyptian Symbols

THE FOUNDATIONAL INTRODUCTION of our framework begins by outlining the most common symbols, such as the ankh, the eye of Horus, and the scarab beetle. It explains their historical significance and evolution, providing a solid base to explore deeper meanings.

## Comparative Analysis and Symbol Interpretation

THE FRAMEWORK SUGGESTS employing comparative analysis to understand the nuances of these symbols. We can uncover unique aspects of Egyptian civilization by comparing them with similar icons in other cultures. This component uses visual aids and interactive exercises to facilitate a comprehensive understanding.

## Application in Mythological Contexts

THE FINAL COMPONENT of the framework focuses on practical application. It guides readers through analyzing texts and artifacts, using their understanding of symbols to unlock deeper narrative layers. This encourages not just passive learning but active engagement with the material.

The dynamics of this model show that as one's understanding of symbols deepens, one's ability to interpret narratives in a more informed and nuanced manner improves. This iterative learning process enhances both knowledge and appreciation of ancient mythology.

*This framework ties together the identification, understanding, and appreciation of symbols, illustrating how they form a tapebrick to decode the rich tapestry of Egyptian mythology.*

As we draw this chapter to a close, it's essential to reflect on the profound journey through the intricate symbolism of Egyptian mythology. The steps outlined here are designed to educate and inspire a deeper engagement with these ancient narratives that continue to fascinate and influence modern culture.

*Step 1: Identifying Key Symbols in Egyptian Mythology* begins with embracing the rich tapestry of symbols that ancient Egyptians used to express cultural and spiritual beliefs. Recognizing these symbols — the ankh, the eye of Horus, and the scarab beetle — is crucial. They are not mere artistic expressions but are imbued with deep meanings, each playing a pivotal role in mythological stories and highlighting the Egyptians' values and understanding of life and the afterlife.

*Step 2: Using Visual and Interactive Tools to Enhance understanding emphasizes* the dynamic way we can interact with these symbols today. By engaging with visual aids, documentaries, and interactive applications, the symbols of Egyptian mythology are brought to life, enhancing comprehension and appreciation of their significance. This step is about moving beyond passive learning; it encourages active participation, where one can manipulate symbols, delve into their histories, and even create personal interpretations through activities like vision boards.

***Step 3: Appreciating the Complexity and Depth of Symbols in Mythology*** invites us to look deeper. It's an exploration that urges us to consider the aesthetic aspects of these symbols and their evolving roles across different contexts and eras. This step is crucial for anyone seeking to understand the layered meanings of these ancient signs and how they shape the mythological tales that still resonate today.

Each step in this process serves a specific purpose and builds upon the last, forming a comprehensive pathway toward understanding and appreciating Egyptian mythology's rich symbolic tradition. This approach does not rigidly bind but rather flexibly guides you through personal exploration, allowing for a unique, informative, and transformative journey.

By integrating these steps into your exploration of Egyptian mythology, you engage in a more meaningful interaction with history. You're not just learning about ancient symbols; you're connecting with them, exploring their relevance to the ancients and us today. This engagement offers a profound appreciation for the complexity of human expression and thought throughout history.

Let this journey be both enlightening and inspiring as you continue to explore the depths of Egyptian mythology and uncover new insights hidden within its ancient symbols. The path is laid out for you to learn, connect with, and carry forward the timeless narratives of a civilization that still speaks to us across millennia.

# Chapter 6: Context is Key - Situating Myths in Their Time and Place

Nefertari stood at the edge of the Nile, her gaze fixed on the slow dance of papyrus boats bobbing in the gentle morning breeze. The river was a vein of life, pulsing through the heart of Egypt, just as myths pulsed through the veins of its people. Today, she was to perform in the annual festival dedicated to Isis, goddess of life and magic, a story woven from the threads of history and belief that shaped every aspect of Egyptian life.

As she adjusted her linen garment and dyed a rich indigo to symbolize the waters of chaos tamed by Isis, Nefertari felt the weight of her role. She wasn't merely a performer; she was a vessel for stories that spoke of creation and kingship, order and chaos—stories that helped her people navigate the complexities of their existence. These myths were not just tales to entertain but were central to understanding societal structures and individual roles.

The sun rose, throwing sharp shadows on the sandstone temples lining the riverbank. In these shadows lay stories, too—of pharaohs who aligned themselves with gods to legitimize their rule and of priests who mediated between gods and men in a carefully orchestrated social hierarchy. Nefertari knew these narratives well; they were as much a part of her as her own heartbeat.

As she silently rehearsed her lines, her mind wandered to last year's festival, when an elder had explained how myths like that of Isis and Osiris addressed existential concerns about death and rebirth.

They reassured people that from decay came new life, mirroring the annual flooding of the Nile, which brought fertility to an otherwise barren desert.

Interrupted by a sudden gust carrying the scent of lotus flowers and fresh earth—a reminder that even nature played its part in this grand narrative—Nefertari refocused on her immediate surroundings. Children played at the water's edge while vendors shouted praises for their wares: figs as sweet as honeyed wine, amulets carved with symbols meant to protect and bless.

As she stepped forward to join other performers gathering near a makeshift stage by an old sycamore tree revered as a living shrine, Nefertari felt a momentary connection across time—a thread linking the past with the present through shared stories. How did these ancient narratives continue to shape modern understanding?

*And what could they still teach us about confronting our own societal challenges*?

# Unveiling the Tapestry of Time: The Power of Context in Ancient Egyptian Mythology

## The Essence of Historical and Cultural Contexts

TO TRULY GRASP THE profound depth of Egyptian mythology, one must first dive into the waters of its historical and cultural contexts. Ancient Egyptian myths were not merely stories but reflections of societal norms, political climates, and spiritual beliefs.

*Understanding these elements* is crucial to appreciating why certain gods were revered, why rituals were established, and why myths shaped the foundation of Ancient Egyptian civilization.

## Myths as Mirrors to Society

THE RELATIONSHIP BETWEEN ancient myths and societal structures provides a fascinating lens through which to view history. These stories offer more than entertainment—they serve as a barometer for societal hierarchy and social norms. By exploring how myths are intertwined with the realities of their times, we gain insights into ancient Egyptians' power dynamics and daily lives. This chapter will delve into how gods like Osiris and Isis influenced concepts of morality, governance, and familial responsibilities.

## Addressing Existential Concerns Through Mythology

MYTHS ALSO PLAYED A crucial role in addressing the existential concerns and societal issues prevalent during their times. These narratives comforted and guided people facing the uncertainties of life and death, prosperity, and disaster. Through tales of divine intervention and cosmic order, Egyptians found meaning in their existence and an understanding of their place in the universe. This chapter will explore these themes, highlighting how mythology served both as an escape from and a confrontation with reality.

## A Journey Through Time

AS WE PEEL BACK THE layers of history, each myth reveals a piece of Ancient Egypt's complex societal puzzle. From the divine right of pharaohs to the commoner's hopes for the afterlife, mythology reflects diverse aspects of Egyptian life. This exploration is not just academic; it's a journey toward understanding human nature itself through the lens of ancient narratives.

## The Lasting Impact on Modern Perceptions

BY SITUATING THESE myths within their appropriate contexts, we preserve their integrity and enhance our contemporary interpretations.

This approach allows us to see beyond the mystique of Egypt's deities and pharaohs—to understand them as subjects deeply embedded in and reflective of their time.

## Forward Into the Past

IN THIS CHAPTER, OUR journey through Egypt's mythic landscape will be enlightening and transformative. From creation myths to tales of resurrection, each story will be reexamined for its narrative and its ability to convey deeper truths about human existence within a structured society.

The insights gained here are more than historical recountings; they are keys to unlocking a deeper understanding of one of humanity's oldest civilizations. By contextualizing these myths, we do not confine them to the past; instead, we allow them to breathe new life into our understanding of history, culture, and human psychology.

## Analyzing Historical and Cultural Contexts

EGYPTIAN MYTHS WERE not merely stories but reflections of the societies that created them. The Nile River, a lifeline in the harsh deserts of Egypt, is akin to how these myths served as spiritual and cultural lifelines to the people. Just as the river shaped the landscape, the prevailing historical events and the culture of the times shaped these myths.

Every myth carried layers of significance, mirroring the complexities of Egyptian society. For instance, the myth of Osiris, which speaks to themes of mortality, resurrection, and justice, was influential during times of political upheaval. It provided stability and hope, reinforcing the idea of an afterlife and divine justice, crucial during change or uncertainty.

Delving deeper, integrating gods like Amun-Ra, revered as a sun and creation deity, into daily life illustrates the Egyptians' attempts to understand and control their environment. This deity's evolution in myths corresponds with the rise of Thebes as a powerful city-state, highlighting how shifts in political power influenced religious narratives.

The myths also adapted to the cultural shifts, absorbing elements from different regions and periods. This adaptability ensured that they remained relevant and reflective of the current societal norms and values, thereby continually reaffirming and reshaping the cultural identity of ancient Egyptians.

*The interplay between historical events and cultural evolution in ancient Egypt profoundly shaped its myths, making them timeless and timely reflections of its civilization.*

# The Relationship Between Myths and Societal Structures

EGYPTIAN SOCIETY WAS intricately hierarchical, and this structure was vividly mirrored in its mythology. Gods and goddesses were often depicted with attributes emphasizing order and governance, resonating with the Egyptians' reverence for a well-structured society.

For example, Ma'at, the goddess of truth and justice, symbolized the foundational Egyptian value of harmony and order. Her presence in myths reinforced the societal importance of these virtues, guiding the pharaohs in their duties as earthly representatives of the divine order.

The myths served as religious tools and a means of communicating social norms and expectations. Through tales of divine judgment and the triumphs of gods over chaos, the narratives fostered a sense of communal identity and shared values among the Egyptian people.

Imagine a society where stories are the threads holding the fabric of community together. In ancient Egypt, myths were these threads, intertwining individual lives with collective expectations and societal roles, much like roots holding the soil to prevent erosion.

The tales of gods interacting with common folk and the pharaohs also served as a reminder of the divine omnipresence in everyday life, ensuring that social norms were adhered to not out of fear but respect for the cosmic order.

*Could understanding these ancient narratives help us reflect on our societal structures today?*

## Addressing Existential Concerns Through Myths

ANCIENT EGYPTIAN MYTHS often grappled with existential concerns such as life, death, and the afterlife, which were central to their worldview. For example, the story of Isis and Osiris deals with themes of death, rebirth, and eternal life, offering comfort and understanding about the cyclical nature of existence.

These myths also addressed societal issues. For instance, the destruction of mankind myth, in which the sun god Ra sends the goddess Hathor to punish humanity for its sins, reflects the ancient Egyptians' concerns about justice and divine retribution, highlighting the moral standards expected within society.

Consider myths as ancient scripts written not to entertain but to offer solace and answers to life's persistent questions. For the ancient Egyptians, myths were like the night sky, full of stars guiding them through the darkness of uncertainty and fear.

Furthermore, myths acted as coping mechanisms during times of distress, such as famine or invasion. They reinforced the resilience of the human spirit and the hope for renewal, much like the annual flooding of the Nile, which brought both destruction and renewal to Egypt.

*We gain a holistic view of their significance and enduring relevance by situating Egyptian myths in their historical and cultural contexts, exploring their relationship with societal structures, and understanding their role in addressing existential and societal issues.*

Throughout this exploration, we have uncovered the profound ways in which historical and cultural contexts shaped Egyptian myths and mirrored the societal structures and existential concerns of ancient Egypt. By situating these stories within their specific times and places, we gain a deeper appreciation of their relevance and the insights they offer into the lives of those who told them.

***Understanding the interplay between myth and society*** reveals how these narratives served as more than mere entertainment; they were integral to maintaining social cohesion and reinforcing the values and hierarchies of the time. This reflection prompts us to consider how our myths and stories function similarly today, guiding societal norms and personal values.

Moreover, by recognizing how these myths addressed existential concerns, we connect on a human level with the ancient Egyptians. Their stories were not just about gods and supernatural events; they also addressed fundamental questions of existence, purpose, and human emotion. This connection underscores the timeless nature of human inquiry and the shared quest across millennia to find meaning in our lives.

As we move forward in this book, let's carry with us the wisdom that these ancient narratives are not frozen relics of a distant past but are dynamic tales that continue to provide insight into human nature and societal development. They encourage us to reflect on our own stories and the contexts in which they are told, reminding us of the power of myths to shape and reshape our understanding of the world.

By embracing these lessons from the past, we are inspired to look at our own world with fresh eyes and a renewed spirit. We are motivated by the knowledge that understanding our history is key to navigating our future. Let us continue to explore these echoes of ancient wisdom, allowing them to inform and enrich our modern lives.

# Chapter 7: Bridging Worlds - Comparative Mythology

In the calm silence of the Cairo Museum, where the whispers of ancient pharaohs seemed to echo off sandstone walls, Sarah stood contemplatively before a display of Osiris, the Egyptian god of the afterlife. The hall was dimly lit, shadows playing across her face as she pondered the deity's significance in Egyptian culture and other ancient mythologies she had studied. Her mind wandered to Greek and Hindu traditions, seeking parallels in their myths of death and rebirth.

Sarah was an anthropologist, a seeker of hidden connections between ancient cultures. Her latest project aimed to bridge cultural divides by highlighting shared mythological themes. Today's visit was no casual tour; it was a deliberate search for understanding, a quest to find universal threads in the fabric of human spirituality.

As she moved through the museum, her footsteps echoed softly on the stone floor. The air was cool and smelled faintly of dust and age—an ever-present reminder of millennia passed. She stopped next to a depiction of Isis, noting her protective posture—a theme resonant with figures like Demeter or Parvati from other pantheons who played similar roles in their respective mythologies.

Her thoughts were interrupted by a group of students bustling into the hall. Their youthful energy contrasted sharply with the solemnity of their surroundings. They gathered around a guide who began explaining the mythological significance of Anubis, the god of mummification and afterlife pathways.

Sarah listened from a distance. Anubis' role as a protector and guide to the afterworld bore striking similarities to Charon from Greek mythology, who ferried souls across the river Styx. This connection sparked an idea in Sarah's mind about how these shared motifs could reflect universal human concerns about death and what lies beyond—fears that transcended cultures and epochs.

She scribbled notes furiously in her journal as more ideas flowed: Could these myths offer modern society insights into dealing with our inevitable mortality? How might understanding these ancient narratives help us navigate our contemporary worldviews on life and death?

As she closed her journal, Sarah looked around at the artifacts surrounding her—silent witnesses to humanity's relentless quest for meaning in life and hope beyond death. Was this deep-seated need for understanding what drove civilizations towards such intricate tales? How might we today draw comfort or wisdom from these ancient stories interwoven with our own existential queries?

# Unveiling the Tapestry: How Myths Connect Us Across Time and Space

IN OUR JOURNEY THROUGH the mystical corridors of ancient Egyptian mythology, we often find ourselves marveling at stories that seem both uniquely captivating and strangely familiar. This intriguing intersection of uniqueness and familiarity forms the crux of our exploration in this pivotal chapter. By engaging in a comparative analysis between Egyptian myths and those from other cultures, we appreciate the artistry behind these ancient narratives and uncover the shared human essence.

The endeavor to bridge cultural divides through mythology is not just an academic exercise; it's a way to deepen our understanding of what it means to be human. *Comparative mythology* opens a window to view the common themes that transcend geographical boundaries and historical epochs. Whether it's the theme of creation, resurrection, or the classic hero's journey, these narratives mirror our collective anxieties, hopes, and ethical dilemmas.

## The Universal Quest for Meaning

WHY DO THESE ANCIENT stories continue to resonate with us today? They speak to fundamental questions about existence, purpose, and destiny that are as relevant now as they were thousands of years ago. In this chapter, we will explore how Egyptian deities like Osiris and Isis find echoes in figures from other mythologies, revealing a shared narrative of life, death, and rebirth that can be enlightening and comforting.

## Discovering Our Spiritual and Social Roots

OUR COMPARATIVE JOURNEY also enhances our understanding of human spirituality and social organization. By examining how different cultures address these universal concerns through myth, we gain insights into the varied yet similar ways societies have navigated the challenges of human existence. This broadens our perspective and fosters a more profound respect for the diverse expressions of human belief and societal structure worldwide.

## Embracing the Dual Lens of Mythology

RECOGNIZING UNIQUE and universal narratives in mythological stories encourages us to view ancient Egyptian mythology through a dual lens. It allows us to appreciate Egypt's cultural heritage's distinctiveness while connecting it with the broader human story.

This dual recognition is empowering—it invites us to see ourselves as part of an intricate tapestry of human history woven with threads of mythic narratives from all corners of the earth.

This chapter aims to inform and inspire through reflective exploration and thoughtful comparisons. By delving into these ancient stories with an open heart and a curious mind, we can find ancient and timely wisdom. In the confluence of past and present, myths cease to be mere stories; they become guideposts for living more meaningful lives today.

In embracing these narratives, we do more than rediscover old gods—we rediscover parts of ourselves. As we traverse this enlightening path together, let us remain open to the lessons these timeless tales offer. By doing so, we continue building bridges—not just between cultures but within ourselves—highlighting the profound impact that understanding our past has on crafting our future.

## Engaging with Comparative Analysis

EXPLORING ANCIENT EGYPTIAN mythology quickly uncovers themes that resonate across varied cultural landscapes. For instance, Egyptian beliefs about the afterlife and judgment closely parallel ideas seen in other ancient civilizations. The Egyptians believed that the deceased's heart was weighed against the feather of Ma'at, representing truth and justice. A similar notion exists in the ancient Greek myth of Minos, who judges the dead.

The comparative analysis process acts like a mirror, reflecting the unique traits of each culture and the shared human experience.

Through this reflection, we recognize our collective hopes, fears, and ethical concerns woven into the myths we have created. Just as different mirrors can reflect the same object with subtle variations, so can examining myths from multiple cultures reveal a multifaceted view of human nature.

Moreover, myths from both the Norse and Egyptian traditions feature a complex pantheon of gods who interact with humanity in instructive ways. Odin, the all-father of the Norse gods, shares characteristics with Osiris, the Egyptian god of the afterlife. Both deities play crucial roles in the governance of the cosmos and human morality, showing how societies use gods to embody their ideals and explain natural phenomena.

By drawing these connections, we enrich our understanding of each myth and bridge cultural divides. Exploring these narratives side by side reminds us that while our expressions may differ, the underlying themes of life, death, morality, and chaos are universally shared.

*Through comparative analysis, we uncover the common threads that connect different cultures, highlighting universal human experiences.*

# Understanding Human Spirituality and Social Organization

EXPLORING MYTHOLOGICAL themes provides profound insights into human spirituality and the structure of ancient societies. Egyptian myths, emphasizing the afterlife and divine justice, reflect a society deeply concerned with moral integrity and the cosmic order. This concern is mirrored in the Hindu beliefs of karma and reincarnation, suggesting a universal question of what happens after we die.

Why do these similarities occur? They speak to a shared human condition, a quest to understand the unknown, and to find justice in the cosmos. Each culture's myths serve as a societal compass, guiding people's behaviors and helping to maintain social order.

This guidance is evident in the tales of heroes and gods, whose adventures and misadventures teach lessons about virtue, wisdom, and the consequences of hubris.

Moreover, the deities themselves often represent natural forces or human traits, illustrating how societies personify their world to better comprehend it. The storm god Set in Egyptian mythology and the thunder god Thor in Norse myth both personify nature's chaotic and destructive forces, demonstrating how different cultures process and adapt to the challenges posed by their environments.

Through these narratives, we gain insights into the spiritual beliefs of these cultures, their social structures, and how they resolved conflicts and maintained order. These stories were not mere entertainment but integral to educating and unifying the community.

*Could understanding these ancient narratives help us navigate our modern complexities?*

# Recognizing Universal and Unique Narratives

MYTHS SERVE AS THE narrative backbone of cultures, encapsulating their most profound truths and aspirations. When we compare myths from various cultures, like those of Egypt and Greece, we note universal themes such as creation, destruction, and redemption. Yet, each culture's flavor is distinct, shaped by its geography, history, and collective psyche.

For instance, the Egyptian creation myth centers around the god Atum, who emerges from the chaotic waters to create the world.

This theme of order from chaos is also present in the Chinese myth of Pangu, who separates yin from yang to form the earth and the sky. While unique in detail, these stories underscore a universal human curiosity about the origins of existence and the forces that shape our world.

However, what makes each myth unique are the specific lessons it teaches about the values and priorities of the culture from which it springs. Egyptian myths often focus on harmony and justice, reflecting their structured, hierarchical society. In contrast, Greek myths frequently explore themes of heroism and individuality, echoing the Greek ideals of personal excellence and civic duty.

*By recognizing these myths' unique and universal aspects, we gain a richer, more nuanced appreciation of humanity's diverse yet shared heritage.*

*This exploration enables us to bridge cultural divides, deepen our understanding of human spirituality and social organization, and appreciate the unique and universal narratives that myths from various cultures offer.*

In our exploration of comparative mythology, we've journeyed through a rich tapestry of narratives that underscore the interconnectedness of human experiences across different cultures.

By examining Egyptian myths alongside those from other civilizations, we've uncovered shared themes that resonate deeply with the universal aspects of human life—love, conflict, triumph, and tragedy. These commonalities bridge the gaps between past and present, between us and 'the other,' fostering a profound understanding of our collective spiritual and societal constructs.

*The process of comparative analysis* not only enriches our knowledge but also invites us to reflect on our beliefs and values. It reminds us that fundamental human concerns remain strikingly similar despite the vastness of time and differences in expression.

Through this lens, ancient deities and heroes become more than distant mythical figures; they emerge as reflections of our humanity, offering insights into the enduring questions of existence.

We've seen how these stories do more than entertain—they educate and elucidate, providing frameworks through which societies can view themselves and their world. The myths of ancient Egypt, when held up against those of other cultures, reveal both unique perspectives and shared wisdom. This dual recognition equips us with a more nuanced appreciation of history and its lessons, which can meaningfully inform our modern lives.

Reflecting on these narratives encourages us to consider our own place within this continuum of human storytelling. It prompts us to ask: what myths are we creating today? How will our stories be interpreted by future generations? Engaging with these ancient tales is not just an academic exercise; it's a dialogue with the past that helps us navigate the present and influence the future.

In embracing the diversity of these mythologies, we are reminded of the power of stories to transcend time and place. Let us carry forward the wisdom gleaned from these ancient narratives to bridge worlds and build understanding in our increasingly interconnected global community. By doing so, we continue the timeless tradition of learning from those who came before us, guided by the light of their profound stories.

By actively drawing connections between different mythological systems, we've deepened our understanding and highlighted the value of embracing diverse narratives. This endeavor is not just about looking back—it's about moving forward with a greater awareness of the richness that different perspectives bring to our understanding of human nature.

# Chapter 8: Gateway Gods - An Introduction to Major Egyptian Deities

Amid the whispering sands of a bustling marketplace in ancient Thebes, a young scribe named Menna paused, his hands stained with the vibrant blues and reds of the paints he used to decorate a noble's tomb. The air was thick with incense and myrrh, mingling with the more earthy aromas of clay pots and fresh papyrus. The sun beat down mercilessly on his linen-clad back as he contemplated the divine figures he was tasked to immortalize on stone.

Menna was haunted by the legends of Isis and Osiris, their tales of death and rebirth resonating deeply within him as he grappled with his own loss. His father had passed into the afterlife not a season ago, leaving behind words of wisdom that Menna now clung to like a lifeline. In his heart, a storm of grief and longing brewed, tempered only by his duty to capture these gods who played their part in the cosmic order.

As he sketched out Osiris, god of the afterlife, Menna's thoughts wandered to Horus, son of Isis and Osiris. He envisioned Horus avenging his father's death at the hands of Set, drawing parallels between this divine retribution and his own unspoken yearnings for justice in the earthly realm. These stories weren't just myths to him; they were a mirror reflecting his inner world—his battles, losses, and hopes.

Nearby, children played in the dust, their laughter piercing through Menna's reverie like rays through clouds. They chased each other around an old fig tree whose roots seemed as ancient as Anubis.

This playful scene softened Menna's gaze; it reminded him that life persisted in all its forms despite the omnipresent shadow of death.

An elderly woman approached him then—a weaver known for her tales about Anubis, the protector of graves. "Menna," she called out with a voice that cracked like dry papyrus yet flowed as smoothly as the Nile itself. Remember that Anubis not only guards the dead but also guides them. Maybe he can guide your heart, too."

Her words struck him; they stirred something within that felt both old and new—like discovering a hidden chamber within one's soul.

As she walked away, her silhouette melded with the golden hues cast by an ever-descending sun.

As night drew near and stars began their watchful dance across an indigo sky, Menna felt an unspoken kinship with these deities whose stories he painted day after day. Could these gods offer solace not just in tales meant for tombs but in navigating his real-world pains?

Could understanding these ancient narratives be essential to preserving history and finding personal reconciliation with life's inevitable cycles?

# Unveiling the Mysteries: Meet the Celestial Architects of Ancient Egypt

STEPPING INTO THE WORLD of ancient Egyptian mythology is akin to entering a grand hall filled with the whispers and shadows of gods and goddesses who shaped one of history's most intriguing civilizations. At the heart of these tales are figures like *Isis, Osiris, Horus, and Anubis*, whose stories not only entertain but offer a window into ancient Egypt's spiritual and cultural priorities. This chapter will serve as your gateway into this rich mythological landscape, beginning with these well-known deities.

The fascination with Egyptian mythology is about uncovering past beliefs and understanding how these beliefs reflect universal themes such as resurrection, *justice, protection*, and *kingship*. By exploring the roles and significance of major deities, we start to see the framework of a society that values divine order and moral law above all. Each god or goddess embodies specific aspects of life and the afterlife, making them relatable and their stories perennially relevant.

### *The Cornerstones of Myth: Understanding Their Roles*

*Isis,* known as the mother of Egypt, is more than just a nurturing figure. Her resilience in reassembling her husband Osiris's body speaks volumes about loyalty and determination. *Osiris,* the underworld king, represents rebirth and moral judgment. *Horus,* their avenging son, symbolizes rightful rule and protection. At the same time, *Anubis* oversees mummification and afterlife transition, ensuring safe passage and fairness in judgment.

These stories are not mere legends; they reflect human fears, hopes, and the eternal quest for understanding our place in the universe. They teach us about resilience (as seen in Isis's story), justice (through Osiris's trials), leadership (in Horus's kingship), and integrity (from Anubis's impartiality). Engaging with these narratives offers more than historical insight; it provides life lessons that are as applicable today as they were thousands of years ago.

# Foundations for Deeper Exploration

THIS CHAPTER BEGINS with these familiar figures and sets a foundation for a deeper exploration of Egyptian mythology. Understanding these central characters provides a scaffold from which the more obscure or complex deities can be understood. It's akin to learning a new language by starting with basic vocabulary before moving on to advanced grammar.

This approach does not simplify mythology but makes it accessible. It invites you to delve deeper into each story, character trait, and symbolic representation with a clear frame of reference. As you become more familiar with each deity's primary attributes and stories, you'll find it easier to understand how they connect with other gods and goddesses within this pantheon.

# A Journey Through Time

EMBARKING ON THIS JOURNEY through ancient Egyptian mythology is not just about studying old texts; it's about connecting with human experiences that transcend time. The themes these deities explore encourage personal reflection—how do we deal with loss? What do we believe about justice? How do we confront our own mortality?

In sharing this exploration, I invite you to consider the historical impact of these myths and their personal resonance. As you learn about Isis's devotion, Osiris's renewal through death, Horus's righteous vengeance, or Anubis's solemn duties, you might find aspects of your life reflected in these stories.

This chapter is your portal into a world where gods walk among humans—not as distant omnipotent beings but as integral parts of human existence, shaping every aspect of life from birth to death. Engage deeply, reflect thoughtfully, and let yourself be inspired by the profound wisdom embedded in these ancient myths.

# Exploring the Pantheon: Isis, Osiris, Horus, and Anubis

EGYPTIAN MYTHOLOGY, rich and intricate, is a tapestry woven with the threads of stories and deities. Among these, Isis, Osiris, Horus, and Anubis stand out as pillars that support much of the mythological structure. Isis, the goddess of magic and wisdom, plays a crucial role in the stories of resurrection and healing. Her husband, Osiris, the god of the afterlife, embodies regeneration and justice. Their son, Horus, represents kingship and protection, while Anubis, the jackal-headed god, oversees mummification and the afterlife.

Imagine a family tree, not of branches and leaves, but of stories and powers, where each deity branches out, affecting the spiritual realm and the daily lives of ancient Egyptians. This analogy helps us understand these gods' interconnected roles, not just in mythology but in fostering a culture steeped in the values they embodied.

Osiris's story is particularly pivotal, highlighting betrayal, death, and rebirth themes. Through his resurrection, aided by Isis's magic, the belief in the afterlife gained prominence. Horus, their son, further emphasizes these themes through his struggles and eventual triumph, which underscore the virtues of rightful kingship and valor.

Anubis, meanwhile, adds another layer to this complex mythology. His role in embalming and guiding souls to the afterlife was critical in a culture that placed immense significance on the afterlife. His presence assured the deceased of a safe passage and judgment, reflecting the Egyptian ethos surrounding death and the hereafter.

*Learning about Isis, Osiris, Horus, and Anubis gives us insights into the foundational beliefs and values of ancient Egyptian culture.*

## Unraveling the Stories: Roles and Significance

THE ROLES OF THESE deities in Egyptian mythology are not just titles or positions; they are threads in the fabric of ancient Egyptian identity. Isis, often depicted as a devoted wife and mother, brings the power of healing and protection in her wings. Her ability to resurrect Osiris with her magical prowess places her as a figure of eternal love and unwavering support.

In the tales where Horus avenges his father's murder, we see the themes of justice and rightful rule played out, echoing the societal values that leaders should aspire to. These stories aren't merely entertainment but moral compasses, guiding the people in values and ethics.

Anubis's role goes beyond mummification. He is a protector of graves and a guide to the other world. His significance is profound. He embodies the Egyptian reverence for the afterlife, a fundamental aspect of their culture.

Thus, each deity plays multiple roles, weaving a narrative that reinforces and reflects the societal norms and beliefs of the time. These stories are mirrors, reflecting the values that held ancient Egyptian society together.

*Could understanding these divine roles and stories be the key to unlocking deeper insights into our lives and beliefs?*

# The Divine Framework: Mapping Mythology

## The Echoes Framework

THIS STRUCTURED APPROACH begins with an introductory segment on each deity. Here, the origins, characteristics, and roles of Isis, Osiris, Horus, and Anubis are highlighted, offering a primer on their influence in the pantheon and among the people. This foundation is crucial for understanding the broader implications of their myths.

The framework incorporates visual and conceptual mapping of relationships between deities. Presenting family trees and networks allows a clearer understanding of divine hierarchies and social orders. These visuals guide the complex relationships, making the connections between deities understandable and accessible.

Thematic exploration is central to this framework. It traces critical themes like creation, justice, and resurrection across various myths, showing how these themes are woven into the fabric of the stories.

This exploration deepens understanding and connects the dots between different narratives and their cultural significance.

Illustrated case studies highlight major myths, focusing on narrative structures, thematic elements, and the roles each deity plays within these stories. These case studies help solidify and apply the knowledge gained, making the myths relatable and relevant.

The dynamics of this framework show how understanding evolves over time. As new archaeological discoveries come to light or as scholarly interpretations change, the framework adapts, offering a flexible yet robust structure for exploring Egyptian mythology.

Practically, this framework helps draw parallels between ancient beliefs and modern-day issues, offering insights into leadership, justice, and moral values. It serves as a tool not just for academic exploration but also for personal and philosophical reflection.

*This framework ties together learning about the deities, understanding their roles in myths, and using this knowledge as a foundation to explore the broader network of Egyptian mythology.*

As we have explored the principal deities of Ancient Egypt—Isis, Osiris, Horus, and Anubis—we've uncovered not just a collection of mythical figures but a gateway into the broader and intricate web of Egyptian mythology. These gods and goddesses are central characters in numerous stories and embody the core themes of resurrection, justice, protection, and kingship that are vital to understanding the cultural and religious landscape of ancient Egypt.

*Starting with these well-known figures* provides a solid foundation for anyone interested in delving deeper into the complexities of Egyptian myths. Each deity's unique attributes and stories offer a fascinating glimpse into the ancient Egyptian worldview and its understanding of life, death, and the divine.

Reflecting on their roles and significance, we see how these deities influenced everyday life in ancient Egypt. For instance, Isis's devotion to Osiris after his murder speaks volumes about the values of loyalty and the belief in life after death. Horus's battle with Set underscores the theme of rightful kingship and order over chaos.

Anubis's association with mummification and the afterlife highlights the Egyptian commitment to caring for the dead, ensuring their safe passage into eternity.

These stories are not just historical or religious artifacts but lessons in resilience, justice, and the eternal struggle between good and evil. They teach us about the importance of duty, the power of redemption, and the endless cycle of renewal. Through them, we connect with the ancients, learning that their hopes, fears, and dreams are not so different from our own.

By beginning our journey with these central figures, we set ourselves on a path to deeper understanding. As we move forward, let us carry the wisdom of Isis, the courage of Horus, the justice of Osiris, and the vigilance of Anubis. Let these deities guide us as we explore the rich tapestry of Egyptian mythology.

By embracing these stories and their themes, we not only honor the legacy of ancient Egypt but also enrich our own lives with timeless insights about the human spirit. So, let us continue to explore, learn, and reflect on these ancient narratives, which have so much to teach us about the past and about ourselves.

# Chapter 9: Together We Learn - The Power of Community in Exploring Myths

As Sarah navigated through the bustling crowd, the sun was already high, casting long, slender shadows across the Cairo marketplace. The scent of spices mingled with the dry desert air, a fusion that tickled her senses every time she walked this path. Her heart beat with a rhythm that echoed the distant sounds of city life, each step drawing her closer to the ancient library nestled in the heart of downtown.

Sarah, a historian specializing in Egyptian mythology, had recently embarked on a quest to deepen her understanding by engaging directly with others who shared her passion. Today was particularly significant; she was to meet with members of an online forum dedicated to Egyptian myths, a group she had interacted with only through pixels and posts.

As she approached the library, her thoughts fluttered back to the heated discussion from last night's forum about the myth of Osiris and Isis. The debate had been lively; opinions clashed like cymbals in an orchestra. Yet, this exchange of diverse perspectives thrilled her – it challenged her views and pushed her toward broader horizons.

Inside the library, Sarah felt a surge of anticipation. The musty smell of old books enveloped her as she walked past towering shelves lined with ancient texts and modern analyses. She touched the spines gently, each book a portal to another time and place.

The group had agreed to meet in a secluded corner on the second floor. As she climbed the stairs, her mind wandered to her upcoming presentation at an international conference on ancient civilizations. Would these new insights gained from today's meeting spark a fresh angle for her speech? How would sharing these discussions influence others' understanding and appreciation of Egyptian mythology?

When she arrived at the designated spot, she found two members already deep in conversation about Thoth's role in maintaining cosmic balance. Their faces lit up as they saw her approach, and they welcomed her into their fold without hesitation.

As they delved deeper into discussions, Sarah noticed how each story shared not only enlightened but also connected them profoundly. It wasn't just about acquiring knowledge but building relationships through a shared enthusiasm for a subject that transcended time.

As the meeting drew to an end and they planned their next gathering, Sarah stepped out into the cooling evening air filled with new ideas buzzing like bees around honey. Walking back through the now quieter streets, she reflected on how community engagement truly enhanced learning experiences—it wasn't just about understanding myths but living them through connections made with fellow enthusiasts.

Could bonds forged over ancient stories be what pull people into history and each other's lives?

# Unlocking Ancient Wisdom Through Community

THE JOURNEY INTO THE past, especially one as rich and enigmatic as that of ancient Egypt, is not merely a solitary trek but a communal voyage that enriches each participant with diverse perspectives and shared excitement. This collective exploration deepens our understanding and connects us with others who share our passion for the myths and legends of yore. In this context, the power of community in learning about Egyptian mythology can be transformative, offering a multidimensional view that is often unattainable in isolation.

# Why Community Matters in Mythological Exploration

ENGAGING WITH OTHERS through various platforms and communities brings an essential vibrancy to studying ancient myths. Whether through online forums, local history clubs, or academic discussions, each interaction weaves a richer tapestry of understanding. These interactions allow enthusiasts to challenge their views, refine their knowledge, and gain insights only possible through dialogue and debate. Here lies the value of community: it acts as a catalyst for intellectual growth and personal connection.

## The Role of Diverse Perspectives

WHEN WE OPEN OURSELVES to the views of others, especially in a field as layered as mythology, we gain more than just additional information; we experience the myths in new ways that can alter our entire perception of historical narratives. This process is crucial for anyone looking to gain a deep, nuanced understanding of topics such as the gods and heroes of ancient Egypt. Learners expose themselves to interpretations they might never have considered otherwise by engaging in discussions and forums.

## Building a Shared Knowledge Base

THE EXCITEMENT THAT comes from shared learning experiences is palpable. It's one thing to read about Anubis or Ra in a book; it's another to discuss these figures with fellow enthusiasts who bring their unique knowledge and enthusiasm to the conversation. This shared excitement not only makes the learning process more enjoyable but also more meaningful. It fosters community among participants, encouraging continuous exploration and discussion.

# Practical Steps Toward Engaging Communities

WHILE IT'S CLEAR WHY engaging with communities is beneficial, knowing where to start can sometimes be daunting. Identifying platforms that cater specifically to interests in ancient civilizations or mythological studies can serve as an excellent foundation. From there, participation becomes key—asking questions, sharing insights, and presenting new ideas or interpretations can all enhance one's involvement and contribution to collective knowledge.

As we delve deeper into the communal aspect of learning about Egyptian mythology throughout this chapter, remember that every conversation could unveil a new fragment of ancient wisdom waiting to be rediscovered. The journey through Egypt's mythical landscapes is infinitely more enriching when shared with fellow explorers who bring their own lights to illuminate the path ahead.

By embracing these communal opportunities for learning and connection, we expand our horizons and contribute to a broader understanding and appreciation of ancient cultures. Thus, every group discussion attended or forum participated in benefits not just the individual but enriches the entire community of learners.

# Exploring Different Platforms and Communities

ENGAGING WITH VARIOUS platforms and communities can significantly enhance the learning experience when diving into the rich world of Egyptian mythology. Online forums, social media groups, and dedicated websites offer treasure troves of information where enthusiasts gather to share findings and interpretations. Here, beginners can learn from seasoned experts who showcase different aspects of the myths, from their historical contexts to their impact on modern culture.

Imagine walking into a vast library, each book representing a different voice and perspective on Egyptian myths. This is what it feels like to join a dedicated online forum: each post and discussion thread opens up new pages of knowledge waiting to be explored.

This engagement enriches understanding and sparks new interests and questions, driving deeper exploration.

Local community groups and book clubs provide a more personal touch. These face-to-face interactions foster a sense of camaraderie and belonging among members who share a passion for Egyptian mythology. Discussions in such groups often lead to lively debates and collaborative learning, where each member brings unique insights.

Moreover, attending lectures and exhibitions related to Egyptian mythology can be profoundly enriching. These events are usually spearheaded by experts in the field and offer a well-rounded, scholarly perspective on various topics, complemented by visual and textual artifacts that enhance the learning experience.

*Engaging with diverse platforms and communities significantly deepens one's understanding of Egyptian mythology.*

## Participate in Discussions and Forums

PARTICIPATING IN DISCUSSIONS and forums is crucial for gaining a broad spectrum of perspectives on Egyptian mythology. Participants bring their backgrounds and knowledge, contributing to a richer, more nuanced discussion. These interactions clarify doubts and challenge existing beliefs, prompting further research and reflection.

Consider the forum a roundtable where each seat is occupied by an enthusiast from a different corner of the world. Here, every voice matters, from the amateur historian to the seasoned archaeologist.

Each contribution adds depth to the collective understanding, making the myths more accessible and intriguing to everyone involved.

Engaging in these discussions also helps identify common misconceptions and lesser-known facts about mythology. It's a dynamic learning environment where correction and support go hand in hand, building a community that values accuracy and insight.

Moreover, participating in forums allows for continuous learning.

As new archaeological findings emerge and scholarly interpretations evolve, discussions in these forums reflect the latest developments, keeping members updated and informed.

Could engaging more deeply in these discussions lead to a personal epiphany about the interconnectedness of myths and reality?

## Foster a Shared Knowledge Base and Excitement

FOSTERING A SHARED knowledge base and excitement about ancient myths through community interaction is akin to fueling a fire. Each shared story or discovered fact sparks further interest and enthusiasm, creating a vibrant, autonomous community of learners.

This communal learning is particularly impactful because it incorporates diverse viewpoints, making exploring myths a more holistic experience. When people from different backgrounds and with varying levels of expertise come together, the resulting discussions are rich with varied insights, providing a fuller picture of the ancient narratives.

Additionally, community interactions often lead to collaborative projects such as online courses, group presentations, or publications. These initiatives deepen the participants' understanding and contribute to the broader field of Egyptian mythology, making it accessible to an even wider audience.

*By engaging with others, we learn more effectively and share in the excitement and wonder of rediscovering ancient myths. This collective journey broadens our knowledge and connects us with others who share our passion.*

Engaging with a community of like-minded enthusiasts enriches our learning experience. It deepens our appreciation for the intricate world of Egyptian mythology. Through platforms and communities, both virtual and physical, we have the incredible opportunity to share knowledge, debate interpretations, and collectively revel in the rediscovery of ancient myths.

***Participation in discussions and forums*** is crucial. It allows us to see through the eyes of others, each bringing their unique backgrounds and insights to the table. This diversity of perspectives helps us challenge our views and often leads to a more rounded understanding of complex subjects. Remember, every question asked and answered weaves another layer into our collective knowledge.

Moreover, fostering a ***shared knowledge base*** creates an infectious excitement about learning. Sharing what we know and expressing our enthusiasm becomes contagious, encouraging others to dive deeper and contribute. This shared enthusiasm makes the learning process enjoyable and more meaningful.

***Reflecting on this journey, it's clear that learning in isolation can never be as fulfilling or profound as learning in concert with others.*** The connections we make, the discussions we engage in, and the collective curiosity we foster truly bring ancient Egypt's myths to life. Let us continue to explore these stories together, supporting each one with insights fueled by a shared passion for uncovering the past.

Let this chapter serve as a reminder of the power of community in learning. Embrace these interactions, cherish the shared moments of discovery, and always remain open to new perspectives. Our quest for understanding can become one of the most rewarding adventures.

# Chapter 10: The Mythology Journal - Documenting Your Mythological Journey

In the golden warmth of a late afternoon, Anna sat quietly at her old wooden desk by the window, her eyes tracing the lines of an ancient text sprawled open before her. The soft rustle of pages mingled with the distant hum of city life as she delved into the intricate world of Egyptian myths, seeking not just knowledge but a deeper connection with these age-old tales.

The room was cluttered with stacks of books and journals, each brimming with handwritten notes and colorful tabs marking significant insights. The air carried a faint scent of jasmine from the small garden outside, occasionally stirred by a gentle breeze playing with stray strands of Anna's hair. As she read about Osiris and Isis, she scribbled fervently in her mythology journal, documenting personal reflections and thematic connections that seemed to bridge centuries.

Her mind wandered to her recent visit to the museum, where she had stood face-to-face with the majestic statue of Sekhmet. The power and mystery encapsulated in stone had overwhelmed her then; now, it fueled her desire to understand the myth and its implications on past and present societies. She pondered how these myths influenced modern views on life, death, order, and chaos.

A sudden chirp from a sparrow on her windowsill broke her concentration. She watched it hop about momentarily before flying off into the fading light. It reminded her of Horus's flight across the sky—an emblem of victory over chaos that resonated deeply with Anna's struggles to find order in life's uncertainties.

As dusk settled over the city, painting the sky in hues of orange and pink, Anna leaned back in her chair, allowing herself a moment to absorb all that she had learned and documented today. Her journey through mythology was more than academic; it was a personal exploration into understanding human nature.

*Could these ancient stories reflect on what it means to navigate modern life?*

# Unveiling the Power of the Pen in Your Mythological Quest

EMBARKING ON A JOURNEY through the enigmatic and rich tapestry of ancient Egyptian mythology is akin to walking through a gateway into another realm. Here, gods and heroes tell tales of cosmic order and offer insights into human nature and ancient wisdom. As we conclude our exploration in *"Echoes of the Gods,"* it becomes pivotal to reflect on how one can internalize these timeless stories.

This chapter introduces the concept of a mythology journal—a powerful tool for those who wish to deepen their understanding and retention of these complex narratives.

# Why Keep a Mythology Journal?

DOCUMENTING YOUR JOURNEY through the world of Egyptian gods and heroes serves multiple purposes. First, it aids in *retention*. Writing down what you learn helps transfer information from short-term to long-term memory, making your mythological exploration more impactful. Second, it enhances *personal engagement*. By recording personal reflections, you catalog information and connect emotionally and intellectually with the material, forging a deeper bond with the myths.

# Strategies for Effective Journaling

IN THIS CHAPTER, WE will explore various strategies for maximizing the benefits of your mythology journal. From structured summarizations to free-form reflection, the aim is to provide you with tools for both rigorous study and personal exploration. These methods are designed to record facts and encourage a dialogue between you and the ancient texts, enabling a richer comprehension and appreciation.

# The Role of Reflection

REFLECTION IS AT THE heart of effective learning. By revisiting your entries and thoughts about different deities and myths, you'll see patterns and themes recurring across stories. This process solidifies memory and allows for an evolving understanding of themes such as morality, leadership, and fate as perceived by ancient Egyptians.

# Synthesizing Myths for Deeper Insight

ANOTHER FOCUS WILL be on how to use your journal to draw connections between various myths and real-world applications. By comparing different stories or gods, you can develop a holistic view of the ancient Egyptian worldview, seeing beyond isolated stories to the broader cultural and spiritual landscape.

As we approach this final chapter before concluding our book, it's essential to recognize how each segment has progressively built up your knowledge base. From understanding individual myths and their characters to recognizing overarching themes and documenting your journey, each step has been crafted to provide a comprehensive grasp on the 'what' and the 'why' behind these myths.

By fostering this practice of documentation and reflection, you're not just passively reading; *you're actively participating* in a millennia-old tradition. This engagement doesn't merely enhance memory—it transforms learning into a personal narrative that resonates with your own experiences and reflections.

Keeping a mythology journal as you navigate through *"Echoes of the Gods"* is more than an exercise in academic pursuit; it's an invitation to become part of the mythological narrative yourself. It's an opportunity to live through these stories, allowing them to inform and transform your understanding of a civilization that has shaped much of human thought. Through this practice, ancient insights are reborn within each reader's journey.

## Implementing Strategies for Personal Insights

WHEN DIVING INTO THE vast ocean of Egyptian mythology, documenting personal insights and connections can be likened to mapping the stars in the sky. Each point of light offers a new perspective, a new story, and a new understanding. Keeping a journal allows you to chart these stories, ensuring no detail is lost in the vastness of the cosmos.

A practical approach begins with simple note-taking. Whenever you encounter a myth that resonates with you, jot down your initial reactions and thoughts. What emotions did the story evoke? Which characters or symbols stood out, and why? This practice captures your raw impressions and serves as a fertile ground for deeper analysis.

As your journal grows, you may notice patterns or recurring themes. The concept of resurrection appears frequently, connecting gods like Osiris with the Earth's natural cycles. Here, your journal becomes an invaluable tool, helping you draw connections that are only sometimes obvious and deepening your understanding of mythology.

To enhance this process, consider using visual elements. Sketching scenes from the myths or creating diagrams to link characters and themes can unlock new layers of interpretation. Visual aids often reveal relationships and details that text alone might not convey.

*A mythology journal serves as a navigator's map, guiding and enriching your exploration of Egyptian myths.*

# Understanding the Role of a Mythology Journal

A MYTHOLOGY JOURNAL does more than preserve information; it actively enhances your engagement with the stories. Like a garden that thrives with regular attention, your understanding of myths deepens as you tend to your journal. Regular entries encourage you to revisit and reflect on the stories, embedding them more firmly in your memory.

This continuous interaction with the material fosters a unique bond between you and the ancient narratives. As you write about your reactions and insights, you're not just a passive reader but an active participant in the ongoing dialogue between the past and present.

Consider the power of repetition in learning. Each entry in your journal acts as a rehearsal, reinforcing details and concepts.

Repeated exposure to the myths makes characters and symbols familiar, almost like friends whose stories offer new meanings with each visit.

But how does this process affect your personal connection to the myths? By articulating your thoughts and emotions, you're conversing with the myths. This dialogue deepens your engagement, making the stories more vivid and meaningful.

*Could this be the key to not just learning myths but living them?*

# Creating a Structured Approach to Myth Analysis

A STRUCTURED APPROACH to analyzing and synthesizing information is crucial to truly grasping the complexities of Egyptian mythology. Think of this process as assembling a puzzle. Each myth is a piece of the puzzle, and your job is to find out how they connect to reveal the bigger picture.

Start by categorizing the myths you read. Group them by themes, gods, or moral lessons. This categorization helps you identify overarching patterns and relationships, much like sorting puzzle pieces by color and shape before attempting to assemble them.

Next, use your journal to compare and contrast different myths.

How does the story of Isis and Osiris differ from that of Seth and Horus? What does this tell you about ancient Egyptian values or beliefs? This comparative analysis not only deepens your understanding but also sparks critical thinking.

Incorporating quotes from scholarly texts or interpretations can further enrich your analysis. These perspectives can provide context and depth, offering a scholarly lens through which to view the myths.

*By documenting and analyzing myths systematically, you build a robust framework that supports a deeper, more comprehensive understanding of mythology.*

This structured approach not only aids in retention but transforms passive reading into an active, engaging learning experience. By recording reflections, drawing connections, and revisiting content, enthusiasts develop a personal relationship with the myths, making each story a part of their own intellectual journey.

## The Journey Through the Myths: A Guide to Personal Mythology Documentation

DOCUMENTING YOUR EXPLORATION of Egyptian mythology through a mythology journal is more than a mere recording—it is an engaging and transformative experience that enhances retention and deepens understanding. Keeping such a journal is a personal archive where insights, connections, and reflections on the myths you encounter are preserved. This practice bolsters memory and enriches your engagement with these age-old stories, making your learning journey both structured and enjoyable.

*Step 1: Establishing the Importance of a Mythology Journal*

Start by recognizing the immense benefits of maintaining a mythology journal. It is a crucial tool for personal growth and self-reflection, allowing you to actively engage with the material and enhance your understanding. Writing down your thoughts can crystallize insights and forge connections between different myths. For instance, noting how the themes of life and death play out across various stories can provide a deeper appreciation of ancient Egypt's cultural values and beliefs.

***Step 2: Creating a Structured Approach to Analyzing and Synthesizing Information***

To effectively analyze and synthesize the rich lore of Egyptian mythology, begin by identifying recurring themes and archetypal characters. Organize your journal entries around gods and goddesses, heroic quests, or moral lessons. This categorization helps you draw connections and identify patterns across various stories, which in turn fosters a more holistic understanding of the mythology.

### STEP 3: DOCUMENTING *Personal Insights and Connections*

Encourage yourself to delve deeper into your personal reactions to the myths. Use writing prompts to reflect on questions like, "How does this myth mirror challenges in my own life?" or "What qualities do I admire in these heroic figures?" Incorporating creative elements such as sketches or diagrams can also visually express your insights, making the journaling experience more vivid and personalized. Regularly revisiting and revising your entries will help you see how your understanding and feelings toward these myths evolve.

Through this structured yet flexible approach, you preserve your journey through Egyptian mythology and enhance your comprehension and appreciation of its rich narratives. This method ensures that each step is actionable and builds upon the previous one, leading to a comprehensive engagement with the myths.

As we conclude this exploration of Egyptian mythology, remember that the aim has been to provide an accessible and engaging pathway into the lives and stories of ancient Egyptian gods and heroes. By documenting your journey, you have not only learned about these figures but have also connected with them on a personal level, enriching your understanding of their enduring relevance. This process has equipped you with the tools to continue exploring, questioning, and appreciating this fascinating mythology, keeping the ancient stories alive in your reflective journey.

# Epilogue

## Embracing the Echoes: A Journey Through Time and Myth

As we draw the curtains on our exploration of ancient Egyptian mythology, I hope that these tales of gods, goddesses, and heroic figures have entertained you and enriched your understanding of a civilization that has fascinated humanity for millennia. The echoes of the past resonate with timeless lessons and enduring wisdom that continue to shape our present and influence our future.

***Ancient myths are more than just stories; they reflect human nature and societal values.*** By delving into the lives of characters like Osiris, Isis, and Horus, we uncover aspects of resilience, justice, and the eternal struggle between order and chaos. These universal themes transcended time and culture and offered valuable insights into our lives and the world around us.

Consider the virtues these ancient figures exemplify in your personal or professional life. ***Leadership demonstrated by pharaohs, wisdom shared by Thoth, or resourcefulness shown by Isis in her quest can inspire innovative approaches to modern challenges.*** Whether you are navigating personal trials or leading a team, the strategic and moral lessons gleaned from these stories can foster enhanced decision-making and ethical leadership.

Throughout this book, we've journeyed together from the creation myths that formed the cosmos to the intricate relationships among deities that governed every aspect of life in ancient Egypt. We've seen how mythology shaped everyday life for ancient Egyptians, providing a framework for understanding phenomena beyond their control.

However, like any exploration of history and mythology, our journey has limitations. Interpretations of myths can vary, and with new archaeological discoveries constantly emerging, our understanding may evolve further. ***Please keep exploring,*** questioning, and researching beyond what is presented here. Egyptology is vibrant and ever-changing, with new findings offering fresh perspectives on old narratives.

I urge you to let the knowledge you've gained act as a springboard for your explorations—whether through travel, continued study, or creative endeavors. Let these ancient stories inspire you to discover more about other cultures, histories, and mythologies.

As we part ways with the gods and heroes of ancient Egypt, carry forward their stories with a spirit of curiosity and reverence. May their trials and triumphs serve as beacons guiding you through life's complexities.

***Remember***: each time you recount these tales or reflect on their meanings, you keep this rich heritage alive in our collective consciousness.

***"History is not just about the past; it is about understanding how we come to think about ourselves in the present."*** – An acclaimed historian.

***May the echoes of ancient Egypt resonate within you long after you turn the last page.***

# Don't miss out!

Visit the website below and you can sign up to receive emails whenever Myrddin Sage publishes a new book. There's no charge and no obligation.

https://books2read.com/r/B-A-JBAOB-BOHBE

BOOKS 2 READ

Connecting independent readers to independent writers.

# **About the Author**

At 67, Myrddin Sage steps into the spotlight as a newly published author, bringing a tapestry of rich life experiences and a vibrant imagination. His journey from a Navy Veteran to a Retired Dispatcher of Messengers has endowed him with profound insights into human cultures and the natural world. As Myrddin introduces his debut novel, he shares a narrative infused with wisdom, whimsy, and a deep respect for the interconnectedness of life. Drawing on his academic background and extensive travels, Myrddin's work explores themes of adventure, discovery, and the transformative power of knowledge. With his first publication, he proves that new chapters can be embarked upon at any stage of life, inspiring readers with the message that it is always the right time to follow one's passions.